MW00389587

Shooting from the Hip

by

Norris Waddill with Nancy Terry

Forward

I learned to shoot in Texas, from my great uncle who grew up in the days when men wore their guns on their hips. I was six-years-old when he told me, “There is no problem shooting from the hip. It’s like pointing a finger at a rabbit. When you are first on the rabbit, pull the trigger.”

One: It's What They Think You Know

On December 8, 1941, I walked into an Army recruiting station in San Antonio, Texas ready to fight for my country, and I wasn't alone, either. By the middle of the afternoon, there were two long lines of eager recruits snaking out of the building and down the streets. Had I known that would be the fastest moving line I'd ever encounter in the Army, I probably would've saved myself some disappointment the first time I stepped into a chow line. I walked through my exams with no problem, which is easy to do when the doctors wave you on without even looking at you. I was ready to go to battle, ready to fight for my country, ready to defend freedom against evil, all within the best branch of the military.

"Raise your right hand," the man in charge ordered.

I felt a surge of pride as I obeyed my first command as a true member of the military. I was ready, ready to swear my allegiance to God, country and Army.

"Repeat after me," the man in charge barked. "And then you'll be in the Navy."

"Hey, man!" I shouted back. "I want in the Army, not the Navy."

"Anybody here who doesn't want Navy, go next door."

I went next door, only to discover that the Army recruiters were locked up for the day. Since I had used up my only day off, I wouldn't be able to get off work for another few weeks. I wouldn't be able to get back to the recruiting station for quite a while. So I went back home, still a civilian, only to discover my doctor had already told my mother I wouldn't be able to pass the examinations to get in the Army because of my medical history. She was glad about that. But, boy, did it throw a kink in my plans! I knew the medical exam wasn't a problem for me, but I didn't want to go against my parents to join up. I knew I'd be drafted after my next birthday anyway, so I waited. My mother and father could tell me no, but they couldn't tell the US government that.

So a year later, on December 21, 1942, the papers were in the mail, and I was soon on my way to Fort Sam Houston. It took a couple of weeks to get through the induction program, which was mostly for dental work, shots, uniforms, and briefings of things to expect. After that, I was on a train to Camp Crowder, Missouri, which is about thirty miles south of Joplin, with a training area extending on south through the Ozark Mountains and Indian Creek.

By the first week of February, we were in a barracks in the mid-afternoon, waiting for other orders or something to happen. We were out of cigarettes, which made the boredom almost unbearable. But at least now we had something to do — go find cigarettes.

As we left, we met a well-dressed man on the sidewalk. "Hey, bud!" I asked him. "Do you know where can a fellow buy a pack of cigarettes?"

He replied, "Yes, bud! Just go to the next street and turn right."

When we got back to the barracks with our cigarettes, I knew I had made my first mistake. The same man who I called, "Bud," was up front, about to speak. "I am Lieutenant Richard Webb, and, yes, I am a movie star. But first I am a stuntman, so if any of you want to take me on, well, come on." He went on to give us a quick briefing of what to expect the next six weeks. He also said we would be first in the big parade at the end of our basic training. Then he looked at me and said, "If you need to get the attention of any one dressed better than you, then you should address him as 'Sir' and salute him. Do not ever call out 'Hey, bud!' to get his attention."

Basic training was six weeks on the drill field, rifle range, and training films in bad weather. On the rifle range, we used the old World War I .30 rifle. By that time in my life, I had taken only one shot with a 12 gauge shot gun; I grew up with a .22 rifle. That 12 gauge had knocked me backwards, so I didn't try that again. Not until basic training, anyway. We shot from the prone position, sitting, kneeling, and then standing, taking ten shots at each position. My score was 84, which translated to "sharpshooter."

Next we shot the Thompson submachine gun. It would shoot .45 bullets, single shot or full automatic. The targets of a German soldier with a gun were hidden in a wooded area and pulled up as each of us walked through the course. As each target came up, I remembered my uncle's words. I looked at the figure's heart, pointed the gun, and shot. My score was 97, which meant "expert." Only two of us in the company qualified shooting the Tommy gun, and we both shot "expert." We did it shooting from the hip.

For the next few days, all I heard from my new friends, who were mostly from the Northeast, was, "How did you learn to shoot like that?"

I told them, "I've been fighting Indians since I was four years old."

They believed the story, which meant I had to keep telling it.

We had only one day with the .30 and .50 caliber machine guns out in the woods with guns mounted on trucks. We shot at targets as we were driving by, getting on a target with the help of a tracer bullet. We were never told about a score or that we had even hit a target — the instructors just put us on the trucks and told us to shoot at the targets as they drove us by them. When I took my turn shooting, I tried to get on target by watching the tracer. My shots came nowhere near any of the targets. It was a waste of time; we needed more instruction.

All in all, the first six weeks of basic training were great. We liked the drill field, though is did seem to be pretty useless as training for a war. I thought it was a waste of time. We never set foot on another drill field until after Hitler took himself out with a gun. Getting the blue ribbon at the big final parade was great, but what good did the drill field do? On D-Day, we didn't go in on the beaches as a drill team under the commands: "To the rear, March! Double-time!"

Walking has never been a good thing for me. When I was two-years-old, I lost over half an inch off my right heel bone. My buddy, Thomas Tome, suggested we should try to get assigned to truck driving. He had made a good living driving trucks, but all I could think about was if I was driving, then I wouldn't be walking. So when they asked me what I had worked at, I told them I drove an old cattle truck. That was good enough for them, so I got the job in the motor pool. I had told another lie; there was no cattle truck back home. It is not good to mislead the Army like that, but it was better than the last time I tried to get out of walking. I once tried to get out of a twelve-mile the hike, by not making my bed one morning. I even left a pair of socks on my pillow for good measure. What I didn't plan on was being put on kitchen patrol (KP), washing pots and pans while the other guys were hiking. Dang! I hated to miss that twelve-mile hike.

A master sergeant was the boss of the motor pool. A first lieutenant was in charge of him, and a bird colonel named Briscoe was in charge of all of us. The scuttlebutt was that the master sergeant had a truck company back home, so the lieutenant was really working for him. How does that old saying go? "You're in the Army now." So far to me, everything in the Army seemed to happen backward, not in order.

At our first motor pool meeting, the master sergeant called me up front and told everyone, "This guy has driven a cattle truck all his life, and you need to watch and learn from him." Then he pointed to a four-ton bobtail Diamond T diesel truck, told me to get in it, back it out, and drive it around the lot.

Then I was supposed to park it back where it was. I thought this would be no problem at all. I got in the truck and noticed right off that this was a lot different from a Model A Ford. I got it started, located reverse, and started backing up. There was a crunching and bumping noise behind the truck, and everyone was waving and yelling for me to stop. As I got down out of the cab, I saw a small two-wheel trailer all torn up behind and a little under my truck. How could I have known a small trailer was hooked to that big truck? I got an earful from the sergeant, and after he backed off a little, I mentioned that if we had a big truck back home, we did not use trailers. He put me back in line, and we continued on with the program as planned.

My first trip in a truck was to follow a unit on a twelve-mile hike and pick up those who fell out and needed help. About the first hundred yards, I saw a lieutenant out sitting on a stump. I pulled over, then walked around to let the tailgate down for him to climb in.

He said, "I'll just ride up front with you, Swift, if it's okay."

The name "Swift" was given to me back in about the fourth grade because I was so slow.

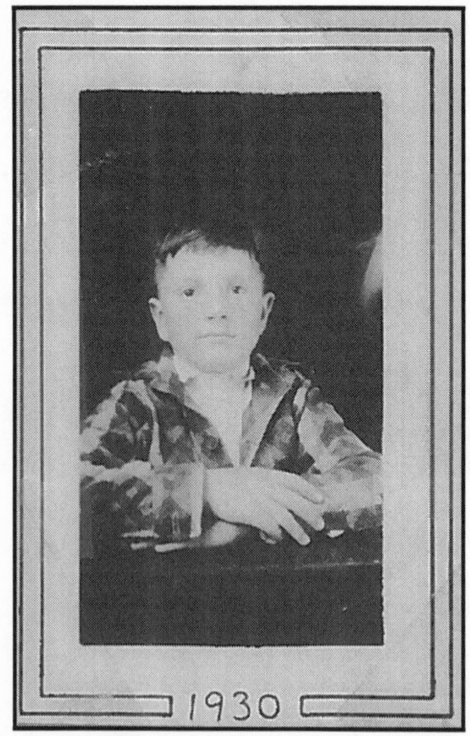

Before he was known as "Tex," Waddill was known as "Swift."

So I'd met this man before, but I sure

couldn't remember where or when.

As we drove on, the lieutenant said he was the Turnersville High School coach from Turnersville in Central Texas. Now that took me way back. I was not good in sports. If I couldn't do it riding a horse, I didn't want to do it. But in my small school, it took all of us to be a team. I had to suit up for football just so we could have a six-man team. The quarterback gave me the ball to go for a touchdown, and I ran toward the goal. I turned and ran out across the pasture. They caught me just before I reached Mustang Creek. That was the end of football for me.

In baseball, the coach told me to play first base, and our first game was at Turnersville. The first hit was a grounder to me. I ran over to get it and missed. The ball went onto right field, and I stood there in disgust and threw my glove to the ground, thinking I had lost the game. About that time, the ball hit me in the back of the head, and I saw all the stars in the sky before hitting the ground. There was no one to replace me. They drenched me with all the drinking water to get me back to life, and the game was on again. We lost that game — and most all of them that year. I'm pretty sure I had something to do with that.

So as the lieutenant got in the front of the truck with me, I asked him if he needed first aid. He said, "No, I'm okay." Neither of us said anything for a while. Then the coach said, "Swift, if you had a choice of walking twelve miles or riding in a truck, which would you do?" I remembered my KP duty and told him I would have figured out a way to miss the hike altogether.

It was about time to start baseball spring training, so I asked if he was coaching.

When he shook his head, my reply was that no one in the Army had asked me to play, either.

He was quiet for a moment. Then he said, “Well, I can understand that.”

That was my first lesson about the Army. It is not what you do; it is what they *think* you do that counts.

Two: Another Man's Name

Eventually, Thomas got sent home. He had been the meal ticket for his mother and three younger brothers and sisters since he was fifteen, so I knew he was needed more there. I did see him years later. He found me and my wife Louise in West Texas two years after the war. We had a good visit, and we were glad to see an old friend.

Working with men in the field was good, but I wanted to be with a unit of a division.

Army vehicles were wired to an on/off toggle switch ignition system. The only way to disable it was to remove the distributor rotor. Anyone leaving the motor pool with a vehicle had to have a trip ticket from the motor pool officer to be legal.

A few weeks after Tom left, I was given a new job driving officers. I didn't like this work at all. I never could understand why they couldn't just drive themselves, and it was a waste of time for me to drive them. I would pick them up, drive to their club, wait, then bring them back, wait, go to lunch, wait, take them to the office, wait, and finally take them home. This went on all day long for one officer after another.

I was assigned to drive a bird colonel. He was a big potbellied man who grumbled all the time and chewed tobacco. He got tobacco juice all over my Jeep. Then he chewed me out for having a dirty Jeep. I know he got a kick out of going upwind of my Jeep to spit. Then he would chew me out again.

In a week or two, they gave us a car to replace the Jeep. Then he had to roll a window down to spit. With the car, he was always on me about the door windows and windshield not being clean. A man at the motor pool told me to put a few drops of oil on a cloth and use that on the windows. I did, and he was right. The windows cleaned up better. The next day, the colonel was ready to spit. The window was so clean, he thought the window was down, but it was up. He made a big motion to spit out the window and plastered his face against the glass, and tobacco juice ended up all over the window and him. He had fire in his eyes when he looked over at me. Then he told me to take him home. I never saw him again, and my next officer was a major who was grouchy and always complained. At least he didn't chew.

My morale went lower when the motor pool sergeant told me I was assigned to part of a cadre group and that I would be at that job until the war was over.

Since I felt so low, this wasn't a good time to write a letter home, but I did. In it, I wrote about sorry gung-ho bird colonels and also a little about majors who were nothing more than the south end of horses going north. I also added that I did not go into the Army to drive unhappy officers around all day. I wanted to go overseas to a unit to help fight the war, not be marking time doing a job that any lady in the Women's Army Corps (WAC) could do.

Waddill at Camp Crowder in 1943

My mother thought it was a good letter and put it in the Gatesville paper the next week. Fort Hood is just down the river a few miles. Someone there got the letter and sent it to the Pentagon. A couple weeks later, I took a forty-eight-hour pass to Joplin and got back Sunday afternoon. All I heard the rest of the day was that every colonel and major in the camp wanted to see me early the next morning.

Colonel Briscoe was first in line. As I reported in, he was looking at papers on his desk. He said, “I believe it is your desire to go overseas,” without even looking up at me.

My answer was, “Yes, sir. That is right.”

Then he said, “Well, you came to the right man this time.” His orders for me were to get on a bus, go home to see my folks, and be back there next Monday at the same time. His clerk would have papers for my transfer to England. These were the best orders I had gotten since I was drafted.

The trip home to see my mother, dad, sister, and all my friends was good.

One thing I learned being back at home was that Army mess hall language was not the best to use around home folks at lunchtime. I did slip up a few times. Just being home was the main thing, though. The crops were all about in, and the cattle and horses were in good shape. My roping horse and I still worked together. Five days went by too fast.

When I returned to camp, there was a memo from the commanding general of Camp Crowder in the recreation room. The last line of the memo read, "Norris, this is a global war, and any job we have here is just as important as it is any other place in the world."

That got my attention.

Was the letter a big deal? I did not see how it could be. As time went on, I began to realize it *was* a big deal. As days went by, I began to hear scuttlebutt that

WAC drivers were taking over so our men could be transferred overseas. Later on the train, on the ship, and in England, it was very common for someone I had never seen before to tell me he had a friend who was out to get me because I had caused him to give up a good job at a camp and go overseas. I really wished no one knew my name at that point.

This bothered me a great deal, even after the war. Then I had a conversation with my stepson, Dick Bellis. He has studied everything he could get his hands on about the Army and US wars since he was very young. He is a Vietnam veteran, wounded twice, once just above the heart, and he still has a bullet in his leg near his knee. When I told him about the letter and the effect it had, his first words were, “That’s the way they did it.” He went on to tell me that at that time of the war, both Eisenhower and MacArthur were looking for a million men each for their wars. So I guess the letter was God's way of letting them know how to get men.

Looking back at the unhappy bird colonels and other officers at Camp Crowder, I wonder if all they had to do was write home about a sorry grouchy gung-ho general they had to put up with and then put the letter in a newspaper near an Army base. I would bet nine hundred dollars to a doughnut that an officer doing that would be catching the next train out with orders to go as close to the front lines as he could get.

My shot record had been lost, so I had to retake them. After a medical exam, I was ready to catch the train to New York Harbor. As we lined up to board, there was a T/5 next to me in line. A T/5 or a "Tech

Corporal" was a Technician 5th Grade which was a specialized corporal. He asked, "Well, Tex, are we ready to go?" I did not know him, but I nodded as we loaded up. I was pretty sure the T/5 was from G2, our military intelligence staff. He called me "Tex," but I'd never seen him before. We mostly played cards on the train. We stopped at a camp near Lancaster, Pennsylvania, to pick up more troops. I guess they had lost their jobs to women drivers, too.

Our last stop was a camp in New York. My buddy Burke left the train to make a phone call, but he quickly came back running, telling me to come with him. At the gate, three beautiful women drove up in a Cadillac. They were Burke's friends and were ready to show us the town. Charlie and I were set up to go to a nearby honky-tonk.

Burke and the pretty ladies gave me a rain check. Charlie, the T/5, and I had a night with standing-room-only sawdust floors and a juke box that played only Ernest Tubb's, "Walking the Floor Over You." I'd been in England three or four months when I learned the T/5 wearing the uniform was a bird colonel. That would've been good to know. Clearly T/5 didn't want us to know he was an officer.

After a few days at that camp, we were loaded onto the Capetown Castle, an ocean liner that was called into service to transport troops.

A twenty-one-day trip from New York to Liverpool, England, was a treat like none other for a young man from Eagle Creek in Central Texas. From that day on, we were in a state of war with blackout conditions and no trash overboard.

The scuttlebutt was that 13,000 of us were aboard the ship, but the ship normally carried fewer than 800 passengers in her normal service before and after the war.

On our trip, there were army cots with hammocks hanging above them from the hull all through the ship. I was in the first one over Charlie Walker's cot in what might have been a storeroom of the ship. With no names on bunks anywhere, no one knew where to find anyone. A gung-ho corporal came looking for Waddill to do KP duty. Only a few folks knew my name; my friends all called me Tex. So I helped the corporal look for me the remaining days of the trip. He never knew I was the one he was looking for. Well… not until we landed in England.

We could see ships all around, and with smooth sailing, that was something. We

Charlie Walker

were flanked on each side by warships. We heard rumors of enemy submarines in the North Atlantic. We were routed up toward Iceland, then back down to the British Isles. The ocean was generally as smooth as silk for most of the trip. We had fair weather, and we saw no enemy subs.

Because of the large number of

troops, the kitchen was open twenty-four hours each day. The short line for chow was between 10:00 pm and 2:00 am. That was when we would generally go for scrambled eggs and marmalade.

One day, we had just started a card game when a man in the room began complaining about a bellyache. It seems we were all having the same problem. Charlie and I went down to the restroom. It looked like there were more than a hundred men in line with more coming. This situation was getting bad in a hurry. It seemed like 13,000 men needed to have a bowel movement, like right now. I told Charlie that this would be a good time to be the latrine orderly. I saw the twinkle in his eye and the smile on his face, and I knew he had an idea of what to do. He took me with him to the latrine door. He told the orderly that Sergeant Jones wanted us to relieve him and that he was to report to the sergeant at the mess hall. The orderly didn't know us and had no reason not to believe us, so he let us take over. There were five commodes. We kept one for ourselves and took turns minding the door and sitting on the commode. The line did not go away until about noon the next day. Did you ever see over a hundred men in line for the toilet when they all had to go really bad? A few did not make it in time. If it had not been for Charlie's quick thinking and the fact that no one knew our names, we would have been some of those who didn't make it through the line.

Another thing my Great Uncle Jeff taught me was to give my name to another man, but not ask for his name because he may not want us to know it. I always thought this was more of a courtesy to the other man, but I was wrong.

Three: Starting Last, Finishing First

The Army camp in Liverpool was a little over a half mile from the ship's dock. The camp, which must have been a stopover for troops, was surrounded by a twelve-foot cyclone fence with barbed wire on top. Charlie and I noticed a beer joint across the street. In England, not only is a beer joint known as a pub, beer is served at room temperature and called "bitters."

Whisky was called "spirits."

There was a ladder leaning on the outside of the camp's fence near the pub. We were supposed to be confined to camp for the night, but Charlie and I had another idea. We had chow and waited for dark. Then we climbed up the fence and down the ladder and were welcomed at the pub. Warm bitters, spirits and Ernest Tubb's, "Walking the Floor over You" went on until past midnight.

When the pub closed, we climbed the ladder and over the fence. Then we could not find our barracks. We saw a light on down a street. There we found a sergeant inside and told him we had been across the street and could not find our barracks. With a big smile, he told us we had come to the right place. He pointed to bunks, told us to get some sleep and said we'd work it out later. About daylight, our captain came to get us, and we were on our way to Norton Manor, the headquarters of Fifth Corps and the Fifty Six Signal Battalion, about forty miles south of Bristol.

When we were standing at ease in formation for roll call, the gung-ho corporal who was looking for me on the ship was beside me and said something like, “Now I’ll find that Waddill fellow.”

When they called “Waddill,” I saw old Gung-Ho looking all around.

I yelled “HEOO” very loud in his ear, and you should have seen the look he gave me.

Then he said, “You son of a bitch, I’ll get you.”

I had to laugh, which only aggravated him more.

Next we were told what outfit we would be in. For me, it was the 1st Platoon of the Headquarters Company of the 56th Signal Battalion. I did not know where Gung-Ho was going. As we were dismissed, he kept saying, "I'll get you. I'll get you."

I walked away, still laughing. Hell, all these years later, I'm still laughing.

First Sergeant Mac walked with me to the barracks I was to be in. On the way, he told me, "Tex, do not write any more letters home."

That let me know a man's record isn't just stuffed in files and crammed in an office somewhere; it's visible. At the barracks, I met Sergeant Stapleton, the platoon sergeant. Even he called me Tex, but I couldn't figure out how they could know where I was from. Then I realized word of the letter I wrote home had gotten to

England before I did.

The friends I had traveled with got split up. Charlie went to 56th Signal B Company.

Headquarters 56h Signal Battalion in Plzen, Czechoslovakia, after the war

We didn't see the T/5 anymore after the ship docked at Liverpool, and that was too bad. He was good-natured and seemed to fit in with the crowd. One of the men who came across with us saw him in restaurant in London once. At that sighting, he was a bird colonel.

He asked about us and said, "Tell Tex hello."

A few weeks later, another man I

didn't know told me of word from the colonel. I always had a feeling that he was in G2 Intelligence or a Secret Service man. Because of the letter I wrote home, I guess they wanted to be sure which side I was on.

This was in late November 1943. I would be twenty-one years old on December 21st. Helium balloons were staked out around all the coastal cities, and with blackout conditions all over the island, there was no doubt we were in a war zone.

English roads were blacktop or gravel, maybe shell near the ocean, and everyone drove on the left side of the road, including us. Our man in the passenger seat was a big help in passing situations on those narrow roads. Since we were driving on the opposite side of the road than we were used to, we needed someone in the passenger seat to tell us when we could pass. I wonder if the English system of driving could have come from the old days of horse and wagon or buggy. In memories of my early days in the 1920s and 1930s, wagon or buggy drivers were normally on the right so they could use the whip on the horses. Most folks were right-handed. The British drove on the left side of the road, but their drivers were on the right side of the car. It seems like the British never realized that there is seldom an occasion to whip a car.

Being in a unit with each of us learning our new duties for the invasion of France was a giant step forward for me. With little or no spit and polish and no more field drills, everyone seemed to be more relaxed and happy with their jobs.

There were fourteen Jeeps and thirty or more men in our platoon. We worked with the message center clerks who handled

O. O. Form No. 7360
(Approved Dec. 7, 1942)
(Old Q.M.C. Form No. 228)

16 December, 1943
(Date of issue)

(Operator's signature)

I CERTIFY THAT Pvt. Norris H. Waddill
(Name and rank)

has demonstrated proficiency in driving (par. 16, A/R 850–15) the types of vehicles listed below as per signed authentication.

TYPE VEHICLE	AUTHENTICATION (Signed by a commissioned officer)
Car, halftrack	
Car, passenger	[signature]
Motorcycle	
Tank, heavy	
Tank, light	
Tank, medium	
Tractor	
Truck-tractor (semitrailer)	
Trucks, cargo, ¼–¾-ton	[signature]
Trucks, cargo, 1½–2½-ton	
Trucks, cargo, 4-ton and larger	
Trucks, amphibian (all)	
Vehicle, wheeled, combat	
Special	

Driver is qualified to drive in the British Isles and on the left hand side of the road.

HQ SOS USAPP 10-43/100M/15496

A British driver's license for a Texas driver

incoming and outgoing mail. All communications from the Army down to every unit at that time had to be in code and delivered by messenger or sent by Morse code on phone lines or shortwave radio. All messengers had to learn both our secret code system and Morse code. The Germans had our code machine but did not know how we set it up for use. We, as messengers, were given those instructions. As I write sixty-six years later, I would still respect that secret and tell no one.

A code section coded and decoded just about everything going out and coming in. Sergeant Hertz was the code man, and Captain Bert was the signal officer. As our troops advanced in the war, there were times that Captain Bert was on the front lines for quicker and better contact. We were there with him to carry the mail when it was ready to go.

Draw a line from Bristol to Salisbury and then to Poole. From that line, go south and west to the ocean. Our units to be serviced were inside that area. We were on call or on duty twenty-four hours a day, which meant we had no other regular duty like KP or guard detail.

During the next seven months, we were learning and doing war games on both land and sea, getting ready for the invasion of France. One day soon after our arrival we were all called out to "police up," which was the Army's way of saying pick up trash. We all spread out to pick up everything that was not tied down. Corporal Trudle was alongside me. A cigarette butt was on the ground by his boot. He told me I had missed a cigarette butt. I told him, "You are just as big and strong as I am, and it is on your side, so get it yourself." One thing led to another, and I was assigned to the mess hall to wash pots and pans from 6:00 p.m. until 8:00 p.m. every evening for the next two weeks if I was not on duty as a messenger. I think that cigarette butt is still there.

Bed check was 11:00 p.m. each night. How was I supposed to wash pots and pans from 6:00 until 8:00, clean up, go to some nearby pubs, and get back by 11:00 p.m.? The only solution was to miss bed check. But each time I missed bed check, I got another week of pots and pans. The company clerk once told me that I would be washing pots and pans through this war and halfway through the next.

One day, all of us who could get loose were called out to run the obstacle course. It looked like half the camp was there, ready to show their stuff. They put us in groups of about fifty that were supposed to go five minutes after the previous group went. Well, there was Charlie. I hadn't seen him for a while. As we visited, we got in the same group, and I saw the first group coming down the fence toward the finish line, maybe three hundred yards away. I showed Charlie and saw that big grin. We managed to be last to go in our group. As the rest turned the first turn, we fell out and went through the bushes to near the finish line. We planned to wait for our group and get in behind them to the finish. But there were two gung-ho men coming around the bend a long way ahead of the others. We came out behind them and ran past them just before the finish line. You should have seen the looks on their faces. They didn't think anyone could outdo them. Then we were known as the two men who started last and finished first. The baseball coach was right. It is not what you do in the army; it is what they think you do that counts.

Once Charlie and I took a twenty-four-hour pass, went to Taunton, and came back in forty-eight hours, just after bed check. On my bunk was a letter from Captain David, our company commander. Everyone was waiting to see what trouble I was in. It was a notice of a good conduct medal. I had the laugh on them, along with several more weeks washing pots from 6:00 p.m. until 8:00 p.m. There was another verse to that song: Charlie had made sergeant, and he got busted back to private.

A couple months later, Charlie and I took a forty-eight-hour pass and came back in seventy-two hours, again after bed check. There was another letter from Captain David. All men in the platoon were waiting, sure I'd finally been busted.

I read it out loud. "We are proud of your work and upgrading you to Private 1st Class." Man, did I catch it from them. One man said he had been there three years, had been good, and was still a buck private. I told him that you've got to mess up now and then so the captain knows who you are.

Charlie was an expert in a crap game. He would never bet much when he had the dice. Then when others had them, he would bet heavy on the side. He would put his winnings in the cuff of his pants leg and roll it up. After his cuffs were full, he would throw all of the money left in his hand on the table and lose the next time he got the dice. He would tell them, "You guys cleaned me out again!" Then he and I would go out on the town. He also sent five hundred dollars home to his wife about every game.

We were on a message run one Sunday. We had stops at the Rangers and also at the Paratroopers. All their men were going double-time, even if they were not on duty.

Everyone thought, "Man! That is the way to go get in shape and be gung-ho."

Well, I thought double-time was stupid. They could leave a little sooner and get there at the same time.

Every day we were on the route that took us to the west coast, then about ninety miles across the moors, and back home. Most of the time, we would run out of gas about halfway across the moors at a roadside park near a creek. So we kept extra gas on the Jeep. Over a small hill, we could see the top story of a sprawling hotel. One day Andy Anderson and I were gassing up, and I told Andy, “It would be a shame if we had forgotten gas and had to wait for gas on the hill in that hotel’s pub.” I’m not saying we actually did that, but somewhere, way back in my memory, I can see Sergeant Stapleton standing in the door of the hotel’s pub door with a can of gas, cussing like a sailor.

Four: Spit and Polish

On all holidays, we went out on war games. Sometimes we were out in the English Channel before making a wet landing somewhere on the beach. At other times we would waterproof our vehicles and drive through vats of salt water deep enough to cover our engine. We had an air intake off the top of the carburetor up by the windshield. We used the lowest gear and drove through at full throttle. If we let up from full throttle, we would pull water back through the tailpipe and kill the engine.

One time, we were on a very large war game with offshore and beach landing. General George S. Patton was with us to observe and judge. After the big show, several thousand of us were crowded around his Jeep, waiting for his comments.

He climbed up on the hood wearing his twin pistols and said, “I have seen all of you in this operation, and very soon you will be landing on the beaches of France. There won’t be a damn one of you coming back.” With those words, he stepped down, got in his Jeep and drove off with his driver as a passenger.

I thought, *Now, that’s the way to go.* All generals should do the driving. Camp Crowder should take a lesson from Patton.

Blackout driving through the moors was another common exercise during holidays. Front and back blackout lights, about four inches diameter, were a fixture on all vehicles. Inside was one luminous light no larger than a half inch that was split top to bottom with a small line. This gave us an estimate of distance between vehicles. As we came near forty feet to another vehicle with these lights, we could see the split lights on each side. Further back than forty feet, however, we saw a single light on each side. With two lights in front and two smaller at the rear, we could miss those coming and going — we hoped. The Army Air Forces (AAF), which were known as the Army Air Corps until June 1947, were known to operate on "a wing and a prayer." In this case, we ran on "a wheel and a prayer." Scuttlebutt had it that the last few trucks of a convoy lost sight of the one in front, took a wrong turn, and went over a two-hundred-foot cliff into the ocean and were never seen again. Could this be true? We didn't know, but it made us a more closely knit convoy.

Roads back then, in England and in America, were narrow. They hadn't been rebuilt wider to accommodate two-way, automotive traffic. One-way traffic was OK, but our army traffic really crowded their roads. Our trucks and equipment with trailers damaged roads and even the buildings and fences, which were on sharp turns. Our men driving large equipment would swing out as far as possible on those corners and still take out part of a fence or corner of a building.

Joe Louis, Joe Walcott, and Sugar Ray Robinson, along with three or four other professional boxers, came by for a couple of days. It seemed like everyone in camp wanted to get in the ring with one of them, but not me. They put on a good show, and we were all glad to talk and visit with all of them. They were all just folks like us. The only difference was that they knew how to fight; we did not.

Donald O'Connor and his sister came by and put on a good show dancing and doing a comedy routine. Everyone thought it was wonderful for them to take their time to come by to entertain and visit with us. To see and visit with world champion boxers and Hollywood stars was a real treat that we will never forget.

One run-in with a general is something else I will never forget. He had one star, I believe, and was the commander of either the 28th or the 29th Infantry

Division. We had just left his headquarters and were driving on the main road. I was in the passenger seat, handling mail and the saddlebags, when we saw the general coming. As we met on the road, I heard him tell his driver to stop, and then he yelled at us to stop.

He stood up in his Jeep and shouted, "Hey, boy! Don't you salute officers?" I didn't know who he was addressing, so I pointed at myself.

"Yes, you!" he yelled back.

I nodded my head, "Yes, I do."

He said I was in deep trouble and rattled on then about how he was going to report me to General Gerow. Then we both drove on our way. Back at camp, I saw Captain David and told him of the run-in with the general. Captain David, being a lawyer, asked me to tell the story as it happened. Then he asked if I was sure that the general called out, "Hey, boy!" I was sure, so he called his clerk in and told him to get my story, type five copies, and add that generals should not address men as, "Hey, boy."

We all signed each one, and they were mailed to both generals and put on record. We never heard from either general. The rumor was when this general was on maneuvers with his unit a couple hundred yards from a beach in a landing craft, he would give orders for everyone to be clean-shaven before they hit the beach. That meant the men had razors in a field pack, salt water, and three minutes or less to shave. Give me a break! This general should still have been in Camp Crowder with that potbellied, tobacco-chewing bird colonel I had to deal with. All that spit and polish never made any sense.

One day in late April 1944, Captain David called a meeting of our platoon. He announced we would be in the invasion of France shortly. Three of us had been selected to volunteer to go in with the first wave of infantry. The volunteers were Sergeant Stapleton, PFC Renner, and PFC Waddill. Since I was one of the newest men, it was a great honor to join those who had been there three years.

If I may take a word from Churchill, that was my finest hour. Stapleton would go in driving a weapons carrier. Renner and I would go in with new Jeeps with center-mounted .30 caliber machine guns. All three of us already had our Thompson submachine guns. We would each have incendiary grenades and shrapnel grenades.

PFC Renner

Our orders from General Gerow were, "Don't stop for anything except a train, and do not look for trouble. If there is trouble, do not be captured. Destroy the Jeep and mail." The reason for not being captured was that we knew secrets of our code system. The Germans did not have that information, and they would do anything to get it. The three of us were relieved of all duty and confined to camp. We had to destroy all personal addresses and pictures of family and friends. We kept only our English driver's licenses and dog tags.

My new Jeep was made ready and waterproof with a T-iron wire cutter up off the front bumper to above the windshield and a large white star painted on the hood. A machine gun was mounted in the center, just behind the seats.

The first trip in my new Jeep was taking an officer to G2, next door to the office of General Gerow. The general came out while I was seated in the driver's seat.

He was looking mostly at the Jeep. As he walked by, he asked, "Do you like it?"

I got out and said, "Yes, sir. I do."

He saw the white star on the hood and the wire cutter and the center gun mount and asked about them. I told him I had just gotten the Jeep that morning, so it was new to me. I would check with the motor pool for answers to his questions. His bird colonel came out and asked the same questions as the general. I just shook my head that I didn't know all the answers. This whole interaction was very informal, more like neighbors who had come by to see a new row binder or a new colt.

As they left, I told them, "It looks like you fellows have covered all the bases. All I have to do is load my guns, and I am ready to go."

They both smiled and went back to their offices. That's when I began to realize spit and polish had no place in combat.

The Germans had a propaganda machine going strong. Axis Sally, the German radio woman, came on the radio at 11:00 every night with top American bands, music, and songs. The night we were selected to volunteer, she called each of our names, ranks, and serial numbers.

Then Sally added something like, “We know you will be coming in with the first wave. Just throw your guns down and come on with us. You will have ice cream cake and a fräulein for the rest of the war.” She also called out our new Jeep numbers, which I didn’t even know at the time. We had no idea how she got this information so quickly. It seems there was a bad one in the crowd, does it not?

My Jeep was set with guns oiled, ready to go. One night after my pots and pans job was done and with nothing else to do, I took a quick shower, sneaked out, and was on a bus to town. I’m not sure why, habit I guess. By nearly midnight, all the places I knew about were sold out of spirits and bitters, so I went into a pub I had never been in before.

Everyone in the place was well-dressed; no soldiers were there at all. I was at the bar having a warm beer. A man came in and sat on the next stool. He began talking about his garden and fruit trees in perfect British lingo. We had another warm beer.

Then, all of a sudden, this Brit was talking like he was from Eagle Creek back home in Texas. He said something like, "Tex, you are in trouble. I must get you out of here."

I knew then this man was in our Secret Service. He told me to be slow and casual while ordering another beer. Then I was supposed to go to the restroom and go out the back door to the alley where he would be waiting in a truck.

When he went out the front door, I did as he said, and there he was with the truck running. On the way back to camp, he told me there were German men in the pub and that I would have been in Berlin by daylight. They would have wanted what I knew and would have started getting me to talk by pulling my fingernails out. If that did not work, they would have started taking my fingers off one knuckle at a time. Then he said they would have started with my family—a sister at home and brother in the Pacific War, Mother and Dad back home near Eagle Creek—just to let me know they could take them out one at a time until I talked.

When we got back to camp, the guard at the gate knew both of us. The Secret Service man did not ask where my bunk was; somehow he already knew. That was the next-to-last time I saw him. I would see him one more time in Paris, France.

Dealing with the Secret Service man reminded me of a training film shown to us in basic training. A Secret Service lady was a singer in a club in Paris, frequented mostly by German officers. She learned locations of ammunition dumps the Germans had in North Africa. She sang a song as a message in code, telling of the locations of ammo dumps. Our air power destroyed them all at daylight the next day, and some say that was the turning point of that war. The song, I believe, was "Lili Marleen," a number one hit in Germany for several months.

As I look back, it is easy to see what a good Secret Service General Eisenhower had working. Besides the T/5 and this Brit, there was also a Navajo Indian in our corps. No one seemed to realize his job was the most important. Now we know the Navajo language was unknown to most of the world back then, and it was being used in Army communication code systems to a great advantage. This Secret Service was able to capture the German who created the jet bomb with wings and a mercury pilot that was bombing cities in England. He was later to be a main man of our space program. I believe these Secret Service people were the beginning of our current Central Intelligence Agency.

I was on duty at the guardhouse one night while waiting to ship out. One of the prisoners started talking to me through the bars. He was in for life but was going to be part of the first day of the invasion. After the war, he would have a clean slate and be free to go. He rattled on for a while. Then he asked me if I had a list.

I must have looked like I didn't understand, so he clarified: "The list of men you are going to take out."

I shook my head. He said there were nine men on his list, and he was going to get them first. I mentioned this to the officer of the day, and I have no idea how all this turned out.

We joined the 1st Infantry Division in southeast England. The 16th and 26th Regiments were the first to go spearhead the beach. We were in one of those; I don't remember which one. As I look back at the army camp in England, I was glad to be with this group of soldiers. We weren't the spit and polish type, but we were trained for jobs to do and were ready to get it over with and go home. Back during the Texas Revolution, Sam Houston had only a few squirrel hunters—my great grandpa was one of them—and they whipped the Mexicans in eighteen minutes and lost only nine men, then went back home. That is the only way to fight a war.

Five: D-Day

June 5, 1944, near 10:00 pm, a message came from Eisenhower to hit the beach at daylight the following morning. We were on the top deck of a LST, a landing ship tank. The ship was anchored portside about three hundred yards out from the beach. We were all milling around saying nothing to no-one as we read the message from Eisenhower. We all knew the hour had come to hit the beaches. As each of us began making our way to join others we were to go in with we noticed other groups climbing over the rail to rope ladders to their landing craft. Each of us knew what to do and we were quietly doing it. This is a picture I will have forever in my mind.

The Navy and Army must have worked extremely well together loading the ship with our equipment. Each vehicle was driven off in the right order. Renner, Stapleton, and I were in the first group to drive out onto a landing barge. Our Jeeps and weapons carrier were in a group closest to the unloading door. My Jeep was loaded with rations, first aid, a few “Mae West” life preservers, gas masks and ammunition. The .30 caliber machine gun mounted in front of the backseat was uncovered and not loaded. Boxes of ammo were open and ready. The windshield was latched down over the hood and covered. Someone had done a good job for me. A pair of old Army saddlebags straddled across the floor boards over the transmission. One bag was for ammo. The other was normally used for messages or mail, but for now, it was filled with first aid equipment.

There were rumors the Germans might use gas. We had changed into new clothing that had been treated to resist gas and carried an odor that was out of this world. We left everything except what we were wearing on the ship. Could this have been the beginning of Army surplus stores? All unloading from the Tank Landing Ship, designated by the military as Landing Ship, Tank (LST) to the landing barges was being done under blackout conditions. Everything was checked, and we were ready waiting to drive out on to a landing barge.

The plan was for the Army Air Forces to meet the enemy ten miles in. Paratroopers were to bail out at 3:00 am. Our combat engineers were to hit the beach at 5:30 am to clean up barbed wire and land mines. The 16th and 26th Battalions of the 1st Division were to hit the beach at 6:00 am. We were to land at 6:30 am. All equipment down below was checked out and ready to roll. I was in deep misery. An avid smoker, I wouldn't be able to smoke until daylight. Chewing tobacco would have been an alternative, but I hadn't been able to find any. Except for the no smoking part, the Army had a good plan.

At approximately 3:00 A.M., we were told to begin loading onto the landing barge. I had studied the maps of our landing area. Our rendezvous point was about a mile or more up on the hill where the road from the beach intersected with a road going north and south near a farmhouse.

A front door from the hull of our ship was let down and became a ramp for us to drive across to a barge. The waves were bigger than fourteen feet. The sailor on the barge warned me they had already lost one Jeep in the water, so I was to watch him for a sign to go. Just before the waves were level with the ramp, he motioned me to go. I drove on the barge as smoothly as silk. Thanks to this sailor, I was on the first row of the port side near the middle of the barge.

We were the last to load. There were about five rows of vehicles with ten or eleven in each row, and we were well armed. Sergeant Stapleton was across on the first row. Renner was in a row between us. My Jeep and all the equipment was loaded for me. I sat with a Tommy gun across my lap and an unloaded .30-caliber machine gun and ammo in a pile of supplies behind my Jeep seat. I could handle the Tommy gun on my lap with one hand if needed and drive with the other. But I had no idea how to load the .30-caliber machine gun. Seemed to me it would have been better if there were two of us—one to shoot and the other to drive. Except for one trip I had taken with Renner, I drove alone most of the first day and night. Having another man working with me would have been a better plan. As I looked back, all trucks and Jeeps on the barge had only one driver. Driving with one hand and shooting with the other didn't seem right; two operators might have worked better. But who was I to question our brass or their plans? I was better trained for the drill field, cleaning vehicles, and looking after potbellied, tobacco-chewing bird colonels.

In the Jeep beside me was a sergeant of the 101st Paratroops. He wore a pistol, had a side mount .30-caliber machine gun, and a bulldog in the passenger seat. I remember asking myself if dogs could shoot a machine gun. I would see him and his dog one more time after the war when we were loading onto a ship to come home.

That loaded Thompson across my lap would shoot seven shots per second on full automatic. A drum of fifty would give me seven seconds before reloading if my math was correct. My orders from the general were to "destroy the mail and Jeep, don't be captured, and stop for nothing except a freight train." I was calm and collected. With the ocean behind me and ships all around, there was only full speed ahead, just a normal day in the Army.

By this time, it was becoming

daylight, but still too early to light a cigarette. A bit later, we were chugging along around in front of the Battleship Texas. It was anchored with her port side about forty-five degrees with the beach and her big guns shooting full-blast. We went around her bow about three hundred yards away from the beach. We were headed north for our landing area, about two or three hundred yards just to the right of the cliff.

Three German fighter planes came in low toward us. Two of them were shot down before they reached us. The third one got hit. I saw smoke coming from its engine. It was headed to crash into the Battleship Texas. My eyes were on the pilot, and I could tell the plane was going down faster than he thought it would. When it became clear he couldn't hit the ship, he banked toward our barge. He stalled between the Battleship

Texas and us and went down.

The first wave of troops had landed, and only a few of the landing craft were on the way back at that time. This could have been because of engine problems. They had become stuck in sand or the operator had been disabled or shot. The scuttlebutt was that the operators of the landing craft were members of a Seabee unit and not regular Navy. At this time, I saw only two vehicles on the beach, and one was knocked out and burning. The other one seemed to be immobile but okay.

Our barge moved toward the beach, and we were about halfway in. German artillery was landing in front of us. Our sailor backed us out a few yards to go in a little to the left from where we were. That was a good move. We learned later that the Germans had the bay divided into numbered squares so when a landing craft came into a square, a spotter would call that number to unleash artillery and shells would rain down. As we were turning back toward the beach, the flagship saw us and headed our way. The sailor told them that we had to move over a little to miss shells coming in.

On a loudspeaker of the flagship an officer yelled out, "What guns are on the barge?"

We showed our guns. They commanded the sailor to "get that son of a bitch in there!" Soon we were moving full speed ahead with twin Johnson outboard motors. A German shell came in and hit the water about six feet from me. Thankfully, it didn't explode.

The destroyer Doyle was three to four hundred yards to our left with her port side toward the cliff. I saw three fires on her deck from all the shelling she had taken. The ship turned, headed out to sea and stopped. Then it went full speed backward, all guns firing at the cliff. At about that time, we beached just to the right of that cliff. We were unloading, and everyone was heading to the right, up a road leading to the hill — the planned meeting area. As I drove off the barge and onto dry land, I saw two of the sailors who had helped us load. They were dead in the water, one on each side of the barge. There was a sergeant who had been hit in the leg and was down. He was dead and had been run over by trucks several times, it seemed.

Before turning to the right, following in line with the others, I remembered a map I had studied of the area. There should be a road up on the hill to the left, I thought. I turned left, up a draw toward the hill. About thirty yards toward it, there was a lieutenant sitting on a rock with his carbine across his knees. I stopped and he came over, stood there a few seconds and said.

"You must be Tex." I nodded.

He said, "I am Lieutenant Engel, your new platoon officer."

I told him to get in and ride. We started up the hill, and he said our instructions were to go to the right and up the road. I told him about a road up on the hill that should take us to the rendezvous area. He went along with that idea. Going up the hill on an impulse was good and got us out of the line of fire and under the cover of the trees. Catching up to the infantrymen was a pleasant feeling. It also seemed to me most of the first wave of landing craft did not come back. It seemed the sailors had been killed or disabled. Trees were the only cover on the north by the cliff. There were no trees in a half moon all around the beach, near a hill to the right of our landing area. The road up on the hill could have been a gift from a God. That got me under cover with men who gave us more firepower. We were not fired upon, and no one in the group fired a gun after we joined up with the infantry men on the hill.

We found the road on the hill and caught up with troops I had been with back in England. One of them yelled out to the others, "Hey, here comes Tex!" Two of them got on our front fenders, and three others got in the back. I put the Jeep in the lowest gear. We were flanked on each side with 1st Division men and went on slowly to the farmhouse with no problems.

One of them made a remark about the unloaded .30-caliber machine gun.

"I only went to shooting drills, not loading drills," I responded. That helped us all relax a little. My new platoon officer told them he would send me to the first machine gun loading school session he could find. Being in a group with that much firepower may have caused the enemy to think twice before beading in on us.

We found the farmhouse and met up with more troops of the Big Red One. They had several German prisoners — one was a young lad, maybe fifteen. He wore the white and red cross of a medic. I was looking at him, and he smiled. Then he walked near my Jeep, still smiling, and eased up closer. Facing sideways, he took a .32 automatic pistol he had hidden under his clothing and dropped it on the floorboard just in front of my seat. Then he got back in line where he had been.

He looked back smiling, and I nodded a “thank you” to him. He should’ve been thanking me – he needed to get rid of the gun before it was found on him because medics should not carry guns.

A master sergeant had a few Germans perched in the loft of a hay barn more than twelve feet up from the ground. They had to jump or die, so they jumped. Some of them lay on the ground unable to get up; the others went off limping. Their officer did not want to jump and was arguing with the sergeant who had a pistol in one hand and a German rifle with a fixed bayonet in the other as we drove up and stopped.

The sergeant yelled, “Jump or die!”

The officer pitched his guns to the sergeant and jumped. The sergeant quickly caught the rifle and put the butt of it to the ground. The bayonet went through the guts of the German officer. I had seen that sergeant in camp while we waited to load out on the ship. He was a career Army man and being in a war was not new to him.

Sergeant Thomas Tubb, a man from my hometown, was in the 49th Combat Engineering Battalion and had led his platoon in the first wave. They had been the first to hit the beach, thirty minutes ahead of all others. They were to clear the barbed wire and land mines for other troops to follow. As Tubb crawled up the hill under fire from the Germans, a one star general who folks said helped plan the invasion came up beside him. The Germans were getting the best of our men in front of them, and they were crawling back down the hill.

The officer pulled his pistol as he and Tubb started up the hill. When they met those crawling down, he yelled at them, "I would rather get it in the face than in the butt!" One by one, they all turned around and took the hill. When I met up with Tubb later during the Battle of the Bulge, he told me this story.

A crippled B26 landed safely in a very small field behind the farmhouse. Captain Bert had just come in and was setting up camp. An hour after our arrival at the rendezvous point near the farmhouse, the first message came in. It was for the Rangers. Two battalions of Rangers had been among the first to hit the beaches, and the cliff was one of their targets. They were to be a couple of hundred yards to the southeast. I took the message, walked toward that area, and found a staff sergeant sitting on a pile of rocks, his gun across his lap. I asked about the Rangers, and he said,

"I am it." He took the mail, and I left with no reply. He was the first of two hundred and fifty who made it to the rendezvous area. There is no way to describe this man as I saw him, sitting on a pile of rocks staring toward the ground, but he is always in my mind. I will see him forever.

Renner and Sergeant Stapleton had come in fine. Our code truck came in and was setting up for business. Since nothing much was going on, we drove out to the crippled B26 that had landed safely. A major showed us through it. That was some airplane. It had everything in a very small space. Men flew in a day or two later to repair the plane and to build a runway of steel two feet wide, the width of the wheels, as a takeoff strip. In only a few days, the plane was ready to fly. It took guts for that major to take off on those strips of steel as a runway in that short field. It took more guts for a man to be in the plane with him. They were back at their base in England in less than a week.

I don't remember much going on until past midday. Near sundown, Captain Bert told me to take a news correspondent who loaded off the LST with him to our code truck to make a report to America. This man was shorter than me and had a round face. I never knew his name. The code truck was out of sight at the end of a field under a bunch of trees. On the way over, he told me this was to be the first news report to America about the invasion. I let the newsman off at the code truck and drove around in the shade under the trees, looking for a place to park. We had clear moonlight. I parked the Jeep and was rushing across the clearing in the moonlight so I could be there and hear his report, and I heard the crack of a rifle and the whiz of a bullet. I knew a sniper was close by, but I was not too worried. I remembered that as long as I could hear the whiz of a bullet, I was fine.

From the back door of the code truck, I heard the newsman begin his report: "The American forces have landed on the beaches of Normandy and have the situation well in hand." I had the door cracked a little so I could hear. I didn't want to hear any more of that stuff, so I closed the door and sat on the steps in the blackout area. I thought, "God Almighty, what is wrong with that man?" Two Panzer divisions were headed our way. They would be here before morning, and we had unloaded very few, if any, armored troops to combat enemy tanks.

The correspondent came out, and I pointed toward the Jeep. He stared across in the moonlight. I caught him by the arm and told him of the sniper, and we both walked around in the shade of trees to our Jeep. The sniper must have moved because we didn't get shot at again. Generally, they move on after firing one shot. On the way back to our camp, we met tanks of the 2nd Armored Division. Then I knew this reporter knew more than I did. I still wonder who that correspondent was.

Scuttlebutt was there was a German lady up on the cliff in a bunker as a lookout for when a ship or barge came into a square. She would call the number of the square to their artillery, and shells would come in. We called them 88s. We believe the Rangers took her out. I also believe the destroyer Doyle did some damage to the hill where she was.

Soon after sundown, Renner and I

were in his Jeep looking for one of our units and came up behind a tank. As Renner drove around to pass, I noticed the tracks were steel. Our tanks had rubber pads.

I said, "That's a German tank."

Renner hit the brakes, backed up, turned around, and dug out. I was looking back and saw that they were pulling over. I told Renner, and he quickly turned across the ditch and into the hedge as far as the Jeep would go and stopped. We were off the road almost through the hedge not seen by those in the tank. The Germans pulled over, stopped and began to spray the road behind us with machine gun fire, and then they drove off. Their guns, which we began to call "burp guns," shot faster than did any of ours.

We drove back maybe a half mile and met one of our armored tanks on wheels. Our guys told us they knew about the German tank and were out to get it. I drove by the next morning and that German tank was still burning, not far from the spot where we had tried to pass it.

Back at camp, things had picked up. We were busy. Renner left alone to deliver mail, and I was alone back in my Jeep. Just like always, we serviced units each in different directions until dawn. On one trip out after it got dark, an officer waved for me to stop. This officer came and stood by my Jeep. My Tommy gun was in my lap, pointed at his gut. He said he was lost and his unit was waiting just off the road ahead of us. He didn't know what to do. He told me he had orders to meet someone who could give him orders. I told him I couldn't help him. He would not let me go without giving him orders of what he should do.

Why he thought I could give him orders, I'll never know. He kept saying that I was from 5th Corps and I should be able to give him orders.

He kept pushing my gun away from his stomach and asking me, "What is that you got poking me in the belly?"

I told him it was my Tommy gun. He got upset and started saying we were on the same team.

"How would I know who you are?" I asked him. "You may be a Kraut."

That got his attention, and he went running off in the dark. I don't know what happened to him or his troops. Maybe he had taken his men off to the bushes. They were not seen there when I drove by later.

Six: The Real Heroes

I returned from a trip at daybreak on the morning of June 7th, the second day of the battle. All troops of our battalion and 5th Corps had come ashore and were coming into camp. Captain Bert gave me mail for General George Montgomery's troops. I asked if he had a clue about where they were. He told me they should have beached yesterday day someplace to our left. I pointed north for clarification, and he nodded yes.

Old Calvary saddle pockets were not normal-issue equipment. We kept them behind the shift lever, one on each side of the driveline box. One was for grenades, and I put the mail in the other. Walter Knight, another man in our platoon, teamed up with me. Man, I was glad to see him. We had great times back in England together. He was a country boy from West Virginia. I was born and reared between Eagle Creek and the Leon River near the middle of Texas. We got along well together; I don't think I ever had a better friend.

As we left to look for Monty and his army, I was thankful once again for studying that map. I knew the road going north would soon turn left toward the beach for seven or eight miles, and the English army should be nearby. As we drove two or three miles north, we met an English command car. General Montgomery was in the passenger seat. As we stopped, he inquired if Eisenhower had shown up yet. We didn't know. We told them we had mail for them and asked where we should take it. Monty told us to stay on this same road a few miles on the right. His men were hidden in the pine trees there.

"You can't miss them," he said. Then he inquired about our troops.

I told him to just stay on this same road a few miles on the right; they were there in the oak trees. "You can't miss them." I didn't realize I had said "can't" like a Brit. I was glad he had a good sense of humor, laughing as they drove off.

Monty was right. We found his men in the pine trees. They were lounging under the trees drinking some kind of white lightning. We gave them the mail, and there was nothing for us to take back. I asked about the drinks.

Their answer was, “Lad, don’t you know that in all storm cellars in France, there are wooden barrels filled with spirits?”

Well, no, I was not aware of that, but it was sure nice to know. The Brit had told the truth. When we got back to our camp, we had seven bottles of white lightning hidden in a ration box. That stuff was really stout. Good advice was not to drink it — just sip it.

When we returned to camp, all of our men had come in and were lying under trees, just relaxing. I was reporting back to the message center, crossing a ditch on the two-by-twelve wooden timber we were using as a bridge. Some of our men from across the road yelled to me.

I stopped on the bridge and yelled back at them. "You would never guess who I saw today!" They were quiet, and I yelled, "I saw that bloke Monty." Then I turned, focusing on my balance. When I jumped to the bank, I fell into General Monty, knocking him backward to the ground. I thought, *God Almighty, I'm in trouble now*!

Helping him up, I said, "I'm sorry about this."

He was laughing and replied, "That's all right, lad. I'm only that bloke Monty." He and his aides laughed. It was good for me he had a sense of humor.

Walter and I were working together again and were out almost all that day and night. As the other men began to learn where all our troops were, we were back to normal. All American troops up to that point had been on the go for four nights and three days. For messengers, that was normal. Our work was mostly all done by daybreak every morning. Then this would start over again around noon.

We were out as far as Saint-Lô. This was the area where the paratroopers were to land after their bailout at 3:00 in the morning on D-Day. Walter and I were returning near daybreak on June 8. Our cooks had set up a mess tent. We were in for chow for the first time since we got there – D-Day was seventy-two hours long for some of us. The chow was great. Our mess sergeant came and sat with us to visit. We gave him a bottle of our white lightning and told him to sip it, not to drink it. Word came to us later the mess sergeant did not sip the white lightning. He drank most of it, got drunk, and whipped up on the mess officer. He got busted and was put on permanent

KP. Later our company doctor came and told us the white lightning was poison and took all we had remaining. We knew he was lying like a dog.

New Year's night of that same year, a lieutenant came and gave us a bottle and said it was stuff he had had for a while and that it might not be good. The first thing Walter and I noticed was the wooden stopper. We had found that bottle, and the white lighting was one of those we took from the farmer's storm cellar the day we met Monty. It was good, not poison. It had just been aged a little longer.

Looking back sixty-seven years ago to how I felt on D-Day, I'd have to say that I was not afraid or uneasy and never once thought I would die in the war. I think it's because of the job our Navy did before and after D-Day. They worked hand-in-hand with us and were a great help in making our job go like clockwork. They lost a lot of their sailors on D-Day, and I don't think they ever received the credit they deserved for their role in that day.

Paratroopers had bailed out about ten miles in. I thought two and a half to three miles in would have been better. Being closer might have gotten the attention of the Germans stationed on the beach. Then we would be hitting them from both sides. But first-class privates seldom are in with four-star generals as they make decisions for invasions.

Captain David, our company commander, had had an appendectomy the day before D-Day, but he was determined to load on a ship. The doctor told him he would miss the invasion of France and would remain in England. Captain David then called 1st Sergeant Mac and ordered him to take him on the ship after the operation so he could go with his men in the invasion of France.

Around the fourth day after D-Day, I was with Renner. We were with troops near the front line. They had captured Germans with their version of our bazooka. The bazooka had been our secret weapon. We put it in the back of Renner's Jeep to take it back to our camp. On the road back, tanks and large trucks meeting us took up most of the road. As Renner pulled off the road straddling the edge of the pavement to miss oncoming traffic, we passed by a telephone pole near the fence. A part of the bazooka extended out and hit a pole. The other end came around, hit me in the left ear, and knocked me out of the Jeep. Later, a medic sewed me up with seven stitches. As I was leaving, he said he needed my name, and I asked why. He said for the records because I would get a Purple Heart. I remembered all the dead on the beach and thought: *For seven stitches?* I shook my head and walked toward my Jeep.

Sergeant Stapleton learned of his brother in the infantry who was dug in on the front line a few miles to the southeast. Those men were to jump attack before daylight the next morning. That would be June 16th. We knew of the attack. We didn't think they did.

So on the eleventh day after D-Day, I drove Sergeant Stapleton and Sergeant Sweeney, our supply sergeant, to Stapleton's brother's unit. We were stopped about a half mile from their camp and walked in. Bulldozers had dug a ditch about ten feet wide and eight feet deep and maybe two hundred yards long. They were putting dead animals in the west end and body bags of those killed in the invasion and later in the east section. German bodies were separated from ours. I saw all of that while Stapleton was inquiring about his brother. That was my last trip there, but the smell of the dead was so terrible that I will never forget it. This was an emergency situation, and the makeshift grave was later replaced by the national cemetery.

Stapleton's brother was surprised to see us. We had a good visit, meeting a few more of his friends in that unit, against the backdrop of the mortar fire that came every thirty minutes. We left just before dark. Stapleton's brother walked with us to our Jeep. Before we drove off, he told Stapleton he would rather be carrying a Tommy gun than his M1. Stapleton handed him his gun and told him he could keep both of them.

The next morning, just after their attack, we got word Stapleton's brother was crossing the creek and was sprayed in the back by a German burp gun. We traced him back to the beach hospital tent. There we learned he had been on a ship back to England and were told he died on the way. Imagine our surprise several months later in Belgium, just before the Battle of the Bulge, when Stapleton's brother came walking into the warehouse where we were bunked. He was fine and on his way back to his outfit. He told us that when he was sprayed in the back, he fell forward on the Tommy gun. He heard footsteps coming, felt a boot tip in his side, and a German turned him over. He said as he turned over, he brought the Tommy gun around and filled the German's gut full of lead. The German fell dead on top of him.

Later, the medics came, and he heard one of them say, "They are both dead. Someone will get their bodies later." He managed to yell at them, and they knew he was alive. After that, he knew nothing. He could not have done that with his M1. The Tommy gun was shorter and easier to handle. It had saved his life. The medics picked him up shortly after that, and he was in the hospital in England for over six months.

We drove by the German headquarters at Saint-Lô. The complex was in a rock cliff and was the headquarters of General Rommel. He was off someplace with his family as we were landing on the beaches. Not long after that, he took the cyanide pill and died. While researching General Rommel, I came across a picture of his funeral procession as it went through

Ulm, Germany.

The first Waddill who came to America was married in the Ulm House in Pennsylvania in 1735. My grandfather was born in New Ulm, Texas in 1858. He grew up in Ox Cart Road in New Ulm, Texas.

Near Saint-Lô were two very large guns. Each one seemed to have been built on a railroad flat car. They were huge and covered the full length of a regular railroad flat car. There were vines growing on them from the ground, and they seemed to be hidden under large trees.

General de Gaulle had begun to build an army of French volunteers. They were set up on the front lines to our left in a tent headquarters. We drove in with mail. The general and another officer were standing inside the gate. He saw our messenger sign in front of our Jeep, and the general pointed to the second tent. That was good. I always figured generals could point better than they could talk. We gave them mail, and there was mail going back to the 5th Corps.

About a mile on the way back, going around a sharp curve to the right, we ran head on into a motorcycle. It was an American Harley ridden by a French soldier. He landed headfirst between us in the Jeep. Our Jeep was not damaged except for the front bumper. The motorcycle was wrecked and lay on the road. We took the man back to the French camp, and General de Gaulle took care of the situation. The man didn't seem to be hurt very badly. I tried to explain the situation to the general, and he told me not to worry about anything. The motorcycle was probably stolen from our camp anyway.

Our work as messengers was

changing. The first few weeks it had been around the clock, day and night. As we began moving through France, our platoon seemed to split into a forward and a rear echelon. Our code truck and Sergeant Hertz and Captain Bert were near the front. Walter and I were among others with them. All others were a few miles back. During slow times, we were all together. Advancing, we became forward and rear echelon. Our work as messengers became primarily nighttime work. All messages had to be delivered before 4:00 A.M. every morning. That meant we were on the road mostly from early evening until daylight. Blackout driving in combat was more of a challenge than daylight driving back in England. Germans would slip through the lines at night and place land mines just under the edge of the blacktop and stretch barbed wire between trees across the road at just the height of our heads, which was a common tactic. Having the wire cutter up on our front bumper paid off. Learning the habits of the enemy had become increasingly important. It seemed to me there were those who were diehard true German soldiers and others who just wanted to slip off and go back home unnoticed. I felt like those diehard soldiers would come through the lines, hide off the main roads all day and then do their damage at night. We learned to recognize anything that seemed unnatural or abnormal. I remember clearly driving at night, hearing the thug of barbed wire being cut by our front-bumper wire cutter.

Generally, men in the code truck had their work done by ten or eleven every night, and we were to deliver all of that to our troops by an hour before daylight. There were some troops moving equipment that needed to be delivered before daylight. Therefore, the larger equipment took the middle of the road. The ditches on each side of the roads were shallow, so we were able to swing out and miss oncoming traffic without much trouble.

One trip I was back at quartermaster for gas, and there were all kinds of Army equipment stacked up in piles covering most of a hill. I saw a stack of paratroopers' boots and told the sergeant in charge I would like to have a pair of size 10½ or 11.

He said, "I can't give those to just anyone; they're special."

Then I told him, "I have a bottle of fine moonshine in my saddlebags, but I can't give it to just anyone—this stuff is special."

The boots fit perfectly.

Another time driving back for supplies we noticed a shower bath complex. It was a string of tents eight or ten feet wide and as long as a football field. Our quartermaster ran this service. We drove up, parked, and took the rotor cap out from the motor. Jeeps had no off and on switch. Taking the rotor to the Jeep would keep it from running so it wouldn't be stolen. Jeeps were a prize vehicle by both our troops as well as the enemy.

At one end of the tent, we stripped down and put all of our belongings in our shoes or boots. An aide took those to the other end. We went through the showers and got new clothing at our last stop. We were cleaned up for the first time and had all new clothing — without the odor of that gas-treated stuff we wore for the invasion. And all it cost us was a few bottle of moonshine.

Nothing unusual happened as we went through eastern France. We learned a little more every day. A German observation plane came over every night just after dark, taking pictures. If anything different showed on their pictures, we could expect artillery shelling to come in. Our air power was in the air day and night. Its battle seemed to be a few miles ahead of us, and only once were we strafed by the Germans. One artillery shell came in and missed my Jeep by about ten feet. It was a dud. The man with me got out of the Jeep and was picking it up to keep as a souvenir as we yelled, "No, no! It's hot!" His hands were burned. We sent that shell back to ordnance. Word came back that it had been filled with sand instead of gunpowder. God must have been with us again. We could thank the factory workers who had slipped sand into the shells instead of powder. That was the second enemy shell to land near us.

Our observation planes also took pictures of the area in front of us. We had up-to-date maps for every move forward almost every day. I later found out about the women who served in our Army Air Forces in England in a documentary. They worked day and night creating these maps using information from our Army Air Forces. I don't know how we got those maps, but we always had them up-to-date and for several miles ahead of our camps.

We saw our old friend Burke from Camp Crowder often and kept him pretty well supplied with moonshine. He was still doing all he could to get in a unit he liked better. He was not happy being with the military police.

We were about twelve miles outside

of Paris, camped out, waiting for General de Gaulle to take the city. Eisenhower held our troops back so de Gaulle and his troops could take Paris. Late one afternoon, Sergeant Stapleton came quickly and told me to get ready; we were going to Paris to deliver a message from Eisenhower to de Gaulle. He said to take all my gear because we would be staying there all night. Our troops would follow tomorrow morning. General de Gaulle had moved his troops in and claimed the city. There were German troops in the northeast part of town as their front line.

We drove in just at dark. All streetlights were on, and everyone was either on the sidewalk or in the street, dancing and drinking champagne or whatever they had. Stapleton and I were the first of our troops to enter Paris, and we got a heck of a welcome. Every time we were stopped by the crowd or traffic, we had to drink some champagne and kiss all the women. Each time, we asked directions to the building where de Gaulle was supposed to be. We found him just before midnight. General de Gaulle had announced plans for a parade the following morning. The message from Eisenhower to de Gaulle was telling him to cancel the parade. The Germans were still at least one division strong in the northwest part of town. We delivered the message, and de Gaulle signed for it. He went ahead with the parade, disregarding the message from Eisenhower. The parade was shot up by Germans as it crossed a river bridge.

After the meeting with de Gaulle, we drove to the Napoleon Dome to camp out until our troops arrived the next morning.

We took the rotor out of the distributor to disable the Jeep. It must have been 3:00 in the morning before everyone stopped celebrating, and we were free to take a nap. We wrapped ourselves in blankets on the sidewalk.

Tex (far right) with group in Paris

We were awakened at daybreak. Two women who lived nearby were kicking us on the shoulders. Their names were Winnie and Monique. Winnie told us her mother was cooking breakfast for us. It didn't take us long to wake up; both women were beautiful. Winnie was a tall blonde, and Monique was brunette and shorter. As we began to leave with them, I saw a man thirty or forty yards away on a sidewalk bench.

I said, "Hey, I know that man!

Those with me told me, "Man, you're crazy."

I walked toward him, realizing he was the G2 man who had gotten me out of the pub in England that night.

As I neared him, he remarked, "Well, I see you made it."

I replied, "Yes. How long have you been here?"

He said it had been two weeks. Then he stood up, cussing me in French and acting like, no, he did not have any cigarettes.

I walked backward with something

like "OK, OK." I didn't want to blow his cover. That gave me another clue about our Secret Service. These men working that far ahead of the front lines needed a big bonus, and we could not thank them enough. They were the real heroes of the war.

Breakfast was great with our new friends. They were really wonderful people. Not long after breakfast, our troops began to trickle in one group at a time. The people of Paris came together as one big welcoming committee, crowding streets and slowing traffic. Our equipment came in loaded with hundreds of our new friends on the trucks. Our unit was to set up in the Napoleon Dome complex. Winnie and Monique were with us to meet and greet all of them. A lifetime's friendship was in the making. Five or six years later, Monique became a dress designer. She had fashion shows in New

York. First Sergeant Mac, Renner, and several others lived in that area of New York, and the party was on. I was in the oil fields of West Texas and could not take the time to be with them. Those girls made greeting cards for us at Christmas and mailed them when we were in the Battle of the Bulge. I still have those cards.

Hand-painted greeting card from Winnie

We were very busy. Our units were in all parts of Paris and its suburbs. One afternoon, Monique was with me after my work was done, and she served as our guide to all the old historic places of Paris. I really enjoyed that afternoon. She was very nice to be with, and I thought of her as a special friend.

We lost a good man that first day in Paris. Dale Stuck and Bates were caught in a fight the French were having with Germans, and they tried to find a safer way to get out of that mess. While turning around, they ran over a land mine. We lost Bates. That was a great shock for Dale, who was injured but still able to stay with us. It took quite a while for him to return to normal.

Seven: On the Road

We were in Paris just short of two weeks before we moved out, driving North by the Arc de Triomphe. The 5th Armored Division, which came in with us, was heading northeast out of Paris. I noticed a Jeep parked in front of a hotel as we drove out of town. A plate on the front bumper had two stars and the 5th Armored Division sign. A person might think there was a major general nearby.

Only the forward echelon was moving out; all the others would stay in Paris longer. We found ourselves very busy. We had to split up and go alone. During one session, I was in my Jeep for two-and-half days straight. My right leg became swollen, and there was no feeling below my hip. This was caused by the operation on my foot I'd had as a child. My right foot rested at an uncomfortable angle on the pedals because doctors took about a half-inch off my right heel bone. At the message center, they gave me more mail for another trip. I told them I couldn't drive, that I needed to get out of the Jeep for a while. They argued that there was no one else who knew where the troops were. I walked out, took the rotor cap out of my Jeep, pitched a tent, took a big sip of cognac, and went to sleep.

A short time later, Captain Lunine

came and woke me. He was our doctor. He looked at my leg and foot and told me that I would be going home, that I should not be in the Army with a foot like that. We had a few more words. Then I told him I had the rotor cap of my Jeep in my pocket, and I was not going home. I would be OK and would catch up with my outfit tomorrow, so he could get out of my tent and leave me alone. He left, and I was fine by noon the next day. I found a small rock to put on the floorboard to give my foot a better angle as I was driving. I found the message center with no trouble and was back at work.

Walter Knight teamed up with me a day or two later. We were near the front, in the area of the dragon's teeth barrier Hitler had built in northern France.

As we forded a creek, we saw a bar not fifty yards from the bank. We stopped and took the rotor cap out of the Jeep, got the saddle pockets, and entered the bar.

Walter Knight

One of the most beautiful women I had ever seen was standing on a table behind the bar taking a German flag down. She had an American flag draped over her arm to replace the German one. We helped her with the flags and then helped her get down from the table. She was the spitting image of Hedy Lamarr, the movie star. She didn't know what we were saying, nor could we understand her, but that made no difference. We enjoyed relaxing for a short time and drove off with two bottles of cognac and lifted morale.

Back at camp, we were telling everyone about the beautiful woman we had met at the bar, and Sergeant Stapleton questioned us about stopping at a bar because he said it was not a good place to park. I told him we would never have stopped there except it had started raining, the roads were slick, and we had slid over into the ditch. Furthermore, a bad thunderstorm had been on the way, and we needed to get the mail indoors and out of the weather to keep it dry. He held his shot glass toward us and said, "Give me one more shot of that stuff."

The dragon's teeth barrier was built of cement pyramids that were placed in rows as though forming a state line. Each "tooth" was about four square feet at its base with flat tops that measured about two square feet. These were set in both directions north and south as far as we could see, with a very small east to west one-way gap for the road through. There were three or four rows of these teeth, creating one line about twelve yards wide. They had been placed so that no type of vehicle could get through.

One night, Walter and I were camped in some pine trees in our pup tent. There was a radio nearby in a larger command tent with sleeping areas. Axis Sally was playing the popular song, "Smoke Gets in Your Eyes." All of a sudden, we heard a burst of gunfire. The music stopped.

We found our Staff Sergeant in the command tent with his carbine across his lap. There was a letter from home on the bunk beside him. The radio had been shot to pieces. He just sat there, staring into space. We heard him say, "She wants a divorce to marry my best friend." Axis Sally had the worst timing.

We followed the troops into Bastogne, Belgium, just before dark one day. Captain Bert and his men set up their code truck system. Walter and I were in our tent nearby. At daylight the next morning, the major general of the 5th Armored Division drove up and went into our message center tent. A short time later, Captain Bert came with mail for the 5th Armored.

He told us "This is important stuff, and they needed it yesterday."

We had no word of them since Paris, and I asked him if he knew about where they should be. He shook his head. Then I pointed to the message center where their general was.

The captain smiled and said, "Tex, you know what to do. Now go do it."

We got the message: the general did not know where his troops were. There was a little humor there, but we didn't know exactly where. We thought the 5th Armored troops were someplace to our right as we looked north. We found tank tracks on a road toward Luxembourg, so we drove south on that road. Every now and then, we would see a tank track. No one showed themselves in towns, which was not normal. Near the edge of one town, we saw an Army ration can. The unusual thing about this was a child, maybe three-years-old, was standing away from the can as it sat open end up. He was in deep concentration, trying to urinate into the can from about two feet out, not even noticing us as we drove by. He was the only person we had seen for several miles in the few towns we had driven through.

About halfway to Luxembourg, we came to a larger town, and there was no one on the street there, either. That was not good. We drove around a curve, and a man stepped out of a hotel and onto the street. He was wearing an Army Air Force officer's uniform. I always drove with my Tommy gun in my lap, which meant that my gun was now pointed at him as he walked up. No one ever noticed the gun, but it was there. We both answered all answers correctly and knew we were on the same side. He had been shot down, and the people had gotten him out of the plane to a safe place before the Germans came. People who were the head of the underground owned the hotel, and he was hiding in a secret room in the attic.

We went inside and met them all. They were glad to see our forces had arrived. They told us the troops we were looking for were camped on a river just northeast of the city of Luxembourg. They asked if we could take the officer back with us, and we said yes, but on the return trip when we were finished with our business with the 5th Armored Division. Our orders as messengers were "do not take anyone aboard the Jeep with us." But this was an abnormal situation, and we took the chance to get this man back home. I must mention that the only child of that couple was a daughter about the same age as our officer. They all seemed to think a great deal of this officer.

On the way down to the city of Luxembourg, we stopped at a bar. As we entered, everyone in the bar walked out. That was not right. We got a couple of bottles and backed out of that bar. We found the general's division and gave the mail to his men and our job was done. Walter saw a guitar in the window of a store in Luxembourg. If I had not stopped so he could buy it, I would have been shot by Walter's friendly fire right there in town. That was no place to die. I stopped, he got the guitar, and we lived happily ever after.

Back at the hotel where the officer was waiting, the family wanted to take their car so they could go with their soldier friend. The family had no gas, so we gave them the two cans of gas we kept in the Jeep. Bringing these people back to camp was really bending the rules. This was nothing new for me.

The first man I spotted was the Padre. He was a bird colonel and always seemed to be around if we needed him. I stopped and told him about our situation. He smiled and told me not to worry about anything. He walked to the family's car, got in with the officer and the family, and we never saw them again.

Walter and I reported to the message center with directions for the general, showing the locations of his division. The general and his driver drove south and a little east. If they didn't get off the main highway and went through the city of Luxembourg to the river, they would find their lost troops.

About twenty years later, *National Geographic* had a picture of that couple in front of the hotel where the officer had hidden on its front cover. The story of their part in the underground was presented in that issue. My friend and coworker in the oil field was Vick. He read the article and told me his mother and father were born and raised in that same town in Luxembourg. His dad was a cable tool driller in the oil field.

As I look back sixty-five years later, I remember that as we traveled across France, we found that the local folks along the roads were friendly. They would want us to stop for a visit. We could not speak French, but the coffee the lady of the house brought us was about two-thirds spirits. A couple of cups of that coffee and language didn't matter. They were fine, normal people just like we were, and they were glad to be free of the Germans.

Andy was with me on a trip the first week on land after D-Day. A couple sat on the front porch with a small baby. They waved, and we stopped. We had coffee and cake with them. Their coffee seemed more than half alcohol. This was legal as long as we took the Jeep rotor cap and mail saddle pocket with us.

Our troops traveled mostly main roads as they pushed the enemy back. This seemed to be the case after Paris. As messengers, we crossed from one main road to another to service these Army units, taking us into more rural areas. Now and then we would see someone who had been faithful to Hitler burning or who had been burned at the stake. We saw more and more of this after we left Paris and later, going through Germany.

Renner and I were out together often.

I liked working with him. He was Catholic, and I was a backsliding Methodist. He would always stop at a Catholic church, go in, and do his thing. He came back all torn up because someone had stolen everything of value that was not tied down.

While in Paris, we saw the cattle cars of a train loaded with people, mostly ladies of the night and Hitler sympathizers being shipped off to Germany.

I must mention that before we left France, Walter and I were in a storm cellar somewhere along the road. We could not find bottles to put spirits in, so we took the barrel, which fit in my Jeep nicely. As we made our normal messenger runs from one unit to another, those we met would fill their canteens. We saw my friend Burke. He was guiding traffic and filled his canteen. On the way back, we drove by, and he was sitting on a stump, very happy to let the world and traffic go by. The next day, Captain Bert told me we had orders from General Gerow. I don't remember the exact orders, but they were to tell that bastard from Texas to get rid of that barrel of whiskey. We didn't need those orders; we were doing just that as fast as we could.

We moved from Bastogne north. We set up in Eupen, Belgium. Our troops were forming a line from northeast of Eupen southwest to Bastogne and on east into France. All the troops were in more of a static front. We were in an area where Army Air Forces bombers and fighter planes were above us day and night. In addition, there were German V2 rockets headed toward London using auto pilots. I may be wrong in calling it a V2 rocket. It was a jet-propelled bomb with wings, guided with a mercury pilot. It had speeds faster than most planes in our Army Air Forces at that time. If our pilots could fly alongside of it and flip it off course with a wing, the rocket would crash. We called these V2 flying bombs buzz bombs. They were set to run out of fuel when they reached England and would explode upon contact. As we drove through remote areas, we saw several of these buzz bombs that had been intercepted by our planes. Our pilot would fly alongside and get his wing under the wing of the buzz bomb and tip it up. That would ruin the mercury pilot. The bomb would go down and explode in the forest.

With a static front, our company had come together. Charlie had made sergeant again. He came by, and we went out on the town like old times. It was great to see him. I saw Burke often, and he was still trying for a transfer into action. Lieutenant Wilson had a brother in the 49th Combat Engineers. They were up front in a forest, camping in a hunting cabin. I took him to visit his brother. I was introduced as Tex. A sergeant on a top bunk asked me what part of Texas I was from. I told him he had never heard of it.

"But I'm from Ireland, Texas," the sergeant said. "I'm Thomas Tubb, and the last time I saw you, we were on a thrasher run, and my wife and I ran the cook shack."

That renewed an old friendship. I saw him almost every day from then on. His job was to clear minefields. The Germans would slip through the lines at night and lay mines. He and his men would search for and disarm them. He was a big help to me. He spoke of tricks the Germans used and things for me to watch out for. Thomas was one of the first men to go in on D-Day to clear barbed wire and mines. He was the sergeant I wrote about crawling up the hill with the officer.

Because we were in a static front, we were entertained by our USO troops. This relaxed atmosphere was not good. The Germans would slip through the lines and lay mines under the edge of pavement. We had snow almost every night, and the Germans would put mines any place on the road and cover them with snow. Fresh dirt on the edges of roads was easy to spot. It could mean the location of a land mine, so we just had to avoid all the humps on the road.

Driving from before midnight until dawn we had problems keeping warm. I traded for coveralls that were regular issue for men in armored units with my old friend at QM. I think they liked dealing with me because I kept the right spirits in my saddlebags to trade. QM areas were generally several miles behind our troops, and nearly all the alcoholic beverages were absorbed by front line troops.

A first lieutenant from the Army came through, staying a day or two. He was out of West Point. He spent most of one afternoon telling me the advantages of West Point officers over those of the ninety-day wonders. As he told me of all these advantages a person has at West Point, I thought if I were going to stay in the Army after Hitler was gone, then I would want to go that way. He was one of very few West Pointers I met, and I must say, he was a step or two above everyone I had met up to then. But as soon as this thing was over, I would be heading back to Texas on the first train out to a boat.

The war was in a lull — nothing much was happening. After being out with Charlie a few hours, I was going back to our quarters in a warehouse. A well-dressed couple walking on the sidewalk tried to start a conversation with me. It seemed they just wanted to be kind to a soldier. We were passing a very nice house. They turned up the walk and made signs for me to come in for drinks. I thought they were nice folks, so why not? I followed them through the front door. With a quick look once inside, I saw a half dozen or more well-dressed men. Four were around a table with papers, and others were lounging. They seemed to avoid looking at us when we entered. I was holding the door open with my left hand and exited quickly, shutting the door behind me. The man or woman did not open the door to see what had disturbed me. As I walked away, a man pulled the curtain at a window, watching me leave. I will always believe this was another attempt by the Germans to capture one of us who knew our code system. We messengers had been briefed that we are prime targets for the German underground system. You could trust no one in a war zone.

Up to this stage of the war, I had been in three Jeep accidents. I've already discussed my last accident, which was with the French soldier on the Harley that we had hit head on. The first was with Renner and the bazooka. Then a few weeks later, I met a convoy sometime after midnight on a dark night. The last truck was a ton and a half, pulling some type of gun on wheels. Because land mines might have been under the edge of the blacktop road, the vehicles were hugging the edge of the road. I was straddling the blacktop edge on my side with my right wheels in the ditch. I didn't see the trailer, pulled back onto the road too soon, and hit the trailer's wheel with my left front wheel. The force knocked that wheel out of line, causing the tire to squeal at high speeds, so we came back to camp more slowly than normal. Our mechanics fixed the wheel in no time at all. They were all from South Carolina and were excellent doing their job, forerunners of our present NASCAR pit-stop workers, no doubt.

Eight: Seasoning the Troops

Just as the Christmas holidays were approaching, we more or less had a static front. Jack Benny had just arrived to put on a show for us. Everything seemed to be calm and collected. I was on a normal message run, with my last stop being the 2nd Infantry Division. They were dug in a few miles southeast of Spa, Belgium, in a pine forest. All of our corps divisions and units were in a line north of this division.

Just after we left the 2nd Infantry Division, a buzz bomb came over, headed toward London. The sun had set, but it was still light as we reported in to the message center. We were told the Germans had attacked about twenty minutes earlier. Could the buzz bomb have been the signal for the attack? We had to go right back with new messages for the 2nd Division. We were stopped just past a railroad track. A warrant officer accepted the mail and took it in an armored tank. When he returned, he said there was fighting in the streets, and the general was directing traffic.

In the line to the left of this infantry Division was the 99th, then the 78th, then the 1st Division, and I believe last was the 29th. The 28th was also in the area. They were all hit hard. I guess the 101 Paratroopers were on R&R. Scuttlebutt was the 99th lost control. Something fell apart, and Germans were getting through. When the 2nd Division general was notified of the situation, he pulled his men off his right flank and covered their spot. This left the right flank open, but the Germans didn't attack the right flank. When we came back to our camp, most of our HQ troops were on the move west to another area. The forward echelon did not move from the compound we were in. We were busy in and out all night and the next day. The Jack Benny show was called off.

We were on a back road near the front when one of our troops came out of the trees toward our Jeep. He wore a 99th Division patch on his shoulder and was running scared. We slowed down a little, and before we realized it, he was crawling up into our rear seat. We pulled over and stopped.

The man was crying, begging us, "Take me back out of here."

We knew this could have been a scam; he could have been a Kraut who had killed one of ours and taken his uniform. A messenger Jeep would be a bonus for the enemy any time. We stayed calm because one thing we noticed was that he was short, stubby and overweight – and any German secret service or soldier would've been in better physical shape – but one of us had a gun on him at all times. We talked with him and decided he was authentic. We drove along slowly and talked him into going back to his unit. He got out of the Jeep and headed through the pasture. This man was not the only one seeming to be out of place. There were a great number of men who needed to regroup and get better organized.

But the Germans were hitting us with all they had, coming at us from the front, and we never realized how many filtered through the lines in plain clothes. We never knew what to expect next.

Our last stop of the second day after the break-through was at our rear camp northwest of Spa. As we came back through Spa, all work was done. We were heading back to our code truck at Eupen around sun-up when I spotted a hotel with a café open for business. There was an alley on one side going to an old-time wagon yard. We drove through the alley to hide the Jeep and walked in the back door. At the bar, they didn't want money; they wanted gas. We brought in two five-gallon cans of gas and set them inside by the door, buying ourselves a fine breakfast. As we left, a bartender gave us two bottles of cognac.

That is one for the saddlebags and the other for the road. Considering we had been in a Jeep for two days, there was no better trade. That morning was the day of the Malmedy massacre. The Germans had a battery of our soldiers, lined them up, and walked down the line, shooting them. We normally took the road between Malmedy and Spa back to our camp, but on that day, just for kicks, we took the north road. The massacre was on the road we normally traveled at about the time we would have reached that area.

Orders came down that all messages leaving our center would be escorted with a .30 caliber machine gun. Renner and I each had a .30 mounted in our Jeep. No others had them in our platoon.

That same day, just after dark, we were escorting Masterson as he entered an infantry camp. A guard came out from behind some bushes as he drove by, raised his rifle, and was getting a bead on Masterson to shoot. He did not see me come up and stop five feet from him.

I said in a low voice, “If you pull that trigger, I will cut into you with this Tommy gun.”

My eyes were on his trigger finger. I saw it begin to relax out of the trigger guard and point straight out. He began to shake, and I swear we could hear his bones rattle. He was really scared. It reminded me of the man in the Bible who got so scared when he saw the writing on the wall. I had always wondered how bones could rattle; now I knew.

The guard settled down on a tree stump and just sat there. I told him that he needed to talk to his sergeant about how to stand guard and that we would be coming out in a little while, so not to shoot us. When we came back out, he was still on the stump, and he did not move as we drove by.

Our bombers and fighter planes were in the air twenty-four hours a day. On the day they called Groundhog Day, all our planes came over. They were bombing everything in Germany that day. All men who were not busy were to be dug in. Naturally, we were on the road most of that day.

Marlene Dietrich, the movie star, was staying in Eupen. Her husband was a fighter pilot in the Army Air Forces. If he was on a mission, she came to our message center and waited for him to send word that he had come back OK. Messages like that could come through our code system. Our code truck was near the main building in the fenced compound with a guard at the gate. A tent attached to the back of the code truck extended about twelve feet, and from that another tent-type waiting room extended another eight feet. A small blackout entry area was at a side door.

One night Miss Dietrich was waiting for word of her husband's return. Frankie and I were on duty, waiting in the lounge area. After she got word that her husband had returned from a mission and was OK, she came out and stopped to visit like always. She was sure a nice lady and always wore an Army Air Forces jumpsuit. As she walked through the blackout area, she stepped on a shrapnel grenade that someone had lost. In a loud voice, she said, "What is this?" and picked it up.

Frankie set it on the ground near the canvas blind and pulled it open, and there she was, bent over and holding the grenade. Frankie and I saw that the pin was almost out. He grabbed Miss Dietrich's hand and the grenade with both of his hands. As he did, we saw the pin fall out to the ground. I started counting. He took one hand off the grenade, got the pin, and put it back in. That grenade would have taken both Frankie and Miss Dietrich out, and I was only less than four feet from them. Thank you, Frankie; you saved the three of us. Many years later, I saw picture of Miss Dietrich sitting on a piano on the cover of a magazine. In the article, she told of visiting troops during the war and having at least one close call.

Frankie and I were alone on a road in the hills a few days later. He never had grenade training and asked what happened if one went off. I told him to get one, pull the pin and throw it. He did and threw it forward. We were driving forward. Good advice: do not throw a grenade forward if you are driving forward. I floor-boarded the gas and pulled to the left as far as I could. We passed the grenade as it rolled off in the ditch. About one second later, it went off. Fortunately we weren't hit. So glad I could help Frankie know a little more about grenade "training on the job."

A letter from home told me my friend Floyd was missing in action. He and I had grown up together. Our families had been friends for the last two generations. Many times after church on Sunday, I would go home with Floyd's family until church that night. His mother, dad, sister, and brother were just like my own, and I loved them all. After the war, Floyd's father died, and his mother was living in town. I stopped by to see her. She was out in the front yard working with flowers.

The first thing she said was, "You

went to see every woman in Texas before you came to see me."

We had a good laugh about that and went in her house for coffee. This was a very emotional visit for me. I told her I had not known Floyd was in the 28th Division, and I had been servicing that outfit two or three times a week. If I had known he was there, we could have gotten together like old times.

Then she asked, "Have you seen Floyd? He's working at that gas station downtown."

That was shocking and good news for me. I thought he had died in the war. A short time later, I was with my old friend again. Floyd told me of his service with the 28th division. They were in the Battle of the Bulge and were camped on a hill for the night. They expected resistance from the

Germans at daylight the next morning. After Floyd got up early and had his gear ready to go, he felt like he needed to have a bowel movement. He walked off from the unit a few yards and had a good old country bowel movement.

Floyd said to me, “You know how a fellow will stand up and take a step backwards and look down to see what he’s done?” He said as he stepped back, he fell off a cliff, and when he woke up, it was daylight. He couldn’t move, and he seemed to be on solid rock in a dry creek. Then he passed out again. Later, he woke up in a hospital in England and was told an old German farmer had found him in the creek and had called the Army. It seems he was unconscious for at least a couple of months and couldn’t remember much of anything when he woke up. No one thought he would make it. He never was told how many bones were broken. Those at the hospital thought he had been through hell and had awarded him all kinds of medals. Shortly after that, he was on a boat coming back to the States. After another long stay in a hospital, he was discharged and on the way home.

We were in Bastogne at daylight one morning after a battle. We had messages for the 45th Medical Unit and two other units in that area. A tent large enough to cover a football field was filled with beds. No one was there, not even sick folks. Then, on the road coming in from Luxembourg, a German convoy was shot up. The lead truck and another large truck were pulled by horses in this convoy. The horses were dead in their tracks. There were three Germans killed, lying across a wagon seat above the cab. The one in the middle was a woman soldier. There was another large truck with four dead horses in front. This German convoy was a half to three-quarters of a mile long. All men, women, and horses had died in their tracks. The entire unit had been hit suddenly and taken out. All trees in the area were stripped, and only a ragged pole stood in the air. This battle had been fought the day or night before.

Further south a mile or two, we located another unit we were looking for to deliver messages. We found no one alive there, either. There were both German and American dead in and around the building. On the way back, we took a road off the main road a few miles out to a unit in a hunting shack. Again, no one was alive there. Again, all the trees in the area were stripped of limbs from bombs and artillery. There were three dead Germans at that camp and more than a dozen dead American soldiers. A German unit of some type could have hit this unit.

Those who have seen action in wars re-live things they've seen over and over. Questions keep coming back. How could three dead Germans and a dozen dead Americans have happened? Think about the war plan of both sides: The Army Air Forces and artillery hit first to soften things up. Then the ground forces struck. This was repeated over and over until the stronger side won. All living things in battle zones are killed. Wars kill all living things; even small crawling things are important to natural life on Earth. We really see and realize the effect of a battle years later when a farmer has to import red ants and other insects to make the cycle of nature complete again. All living things have a purpose.

One night, near midnight, Sergeant Stapleton walked in with his helmet and gun slung from his shoulder. I knew something was up, so I began getting my gear together. I asked if he wanted a man to go with him. He nodded. We were on the way to the door, when Renaldo, another messenger, told him "I'll go with Tex." That released Stapleton. Renaldo and I were headed out. The message was not routine; it was priority so we had to get it delivered to artillery before daylight. A German general was spending the night with a French lady in her château, and our artillery had to take the house and all in it out before daylight. That chateau and our artillery were eighty-five to ninety miles to our southwest across rural roads. That was our destination on a dark night.

Stapleton told us we would be going through areas Patton had just gone through.

There could be Germans, as many as a platoon strong, maybe more. Before leaving, we needed to study a map because normal procedure for messengers was to not light a match or flashlight in enemy territory after dark. Renaldo would not go with me to study the map for roads we could take. He told me to go alone because if we both looked, we might get confused. After an extended study, I had a picture in my mind of roads to the artillery camp. I felt good that Renaldo had that much faith in me, but I would have had faith in his map reading if he would have also studied the map.

Near midnight, we were on the road with our orders. The road seemed to unfold in front of us as we drove. We almost ran over a dark red horse. I hit the brakes, and he whirled the other way. He could see us better than we could see him. There was no other traffic on the road. That was the only traffic we came across for nearly ninety miles.

We drove into the artillery camp about 3:30 a.m. I knew the only way we didn't make a wrong turn all that way was because we had been guided by God. The officer of the day took the messages and told us the cook had coffee in the mess tent. I had not been to this unit for a long time. Going through earlier, we serviced this unit about every day. It was nice to work with them again. I brought the cognac in, which made the coffee better. We learned that trick in the early days in France. A little after 4:00 that morning their man took off on his Harley to their gun locations. Only a few minutes later, we heard every gun in the area going off. We saw the fires burning. The cook fixed breakfast and after that we left for our camp. As we reported in, they gave us thumbs up. Our big guns had taken the general out. Driving back to our camp, I wondered how our people knew about the general and the French lady. Could it have been the work of my friend in the Secret Service?

Walter and I were out early just at daylight again. We were driving up on a hill no more than a mile from our compound when we saw a Jeep burning beside the road a hundred yards on ahead. The driver was in the seat, burning with the Jeep. A bird colonel came crawling out of the ditch on our right and stopped us, fear written all over him. He gave us orders to take him back to the compound.

I told him, "We are messengers and do not turn around for anyone."

He got really mad then and ordered

us to take him back to the compound. I shook my head. He then wanted my name, rank, and serial number. I called that out to him. He wanted it in writing.

"We don't have time," I told him. "Just tell whoever you need to that Tex would not take you back.

As we drove on, he was yelling, "You'll be knocked out."

Our Jeep had a center-mounted .30 caliber, so we weren't fired on. The Germans had gone for cover. German soldiers were just as careful who they would attack as anyone. We were driving in a forest area with trees on each side of the road. If the colonel had been driving and his sergeant had been ready with the .30 caliber gun, they may have not been fired on. We drove on with no problems, taking another road back to camp later that day a couple miles south of where the Jeep was knocked out. About two miles southwest of where the Jeep burned, a major stopped us. He told us we would be fired on if we drove further on that road. There were a bunch of Germans in those trees ahead across the field on the right. The major had what I call a tank on wheels with twin fifties mounted. His Jeep had a side mount .30 caliber. He asked us to wait. He and his men were on a chow break and would escort us through after that.

I asked the major, "Why not have dinner with us?"

They all thought that was funny.

"We set a mighty fine table," I told them.

They just walked away. Walter and I set our rations out on the hood and then set a new bottle of cognac out near the rations. They all looked at the major. Then as they came over, we set out another bottle for them. We all had a fine lunch. The major agreed; we did set a fine table. He kept both of the bottles, but most of the lightning was gone. The major put us between his Jeep and tank on wheels. We drove through as they sprayed the bushes with all they had. There was no return fire from the Germans across the field. They pulled over, and we waved a thank-you and drove on.

There was a bird colonel with the 1st Division HQ. His office was in our headquarters compound. He went out on patrol with the men every chance he had. They said he just loved to be with the men on patrol. Everyone admired and respected him. One morning we drove into their camp. A few hundred yards from our compound, there was a body bag by the guard. The guard told us the colonel had been shot by one of the guards as he returned from being on patrol. This news hit us all pretty hard. Although we did not know him personally, we all had a lot of respect for him. There was no better soldier in the army than this colonel.

New men coming in as replacements and doing guard duty seemed to be uneasy. Those who weren't familiar with the procedures of the unit should not have been called for guard duty. These men, who had only finished basic training, were more likely to shoot first and ask questions later. Then they would have to live with that all the years of their lives. As I look back and remember the war, I realize we were all in adverse conditions most of the time. We, as messengers, drove into unit compounds mostly from midnight until dawn. Most of these units were expecting us because most of the men were seasoned troops. I believe if only seasoned troops were used on guard duty, there would be fewer of our own troops shot. It takes only a few days for a new man to get away from that spit-and-polish stuff, fall in line, and be more at ease with the old troops.

Nine: Winter and Good News

Christmas dinner was a big thing even though the Battle of the Bulge was going on in all directions. The cooks were set up in a huge building. Troops were trucked in from everywhere. Walter and I were in line for the turkey dinner. Those cooks did a wonderful job. Eleanor Roosevelt gave each of us a pair of wool socks. A nearby hospital was filled with wounded and others suffering from the cold weather, and dinners were taken to those patients who couldn't go to the kitchen set-up.

Soon after Christmas, we were doing better in the battle, and our troops were moving out. We were getting more troops into Germany. We had abnormally cold and wet weather. My Jeep had antifreeze testing nineteen below zero. We made one trip with the radiator frozen and drove on back to camp. Our mechanics said the Jeep was not damaged.

We drove into an outpost of the 1st Division and saw a body bag by a Jeep that had been blown up by a mine. They told us that was the old master sergeant. I first met him in the marshal area in England just before the invasion. He had more than thirty years and a lot of battles behind him. He was retiring and was on his way back to HQ to catch a ride home. My thoughts went back to the beach and the barn where he made the Germans jump out of the rafters and then to the officer on the ground with the bayonet through his guts. Neither one of those guys were going to get to go home. I thought what goes around comes around. This was a sad time for all of us who knew him.

We saw my hometown friend Thomas Tubb about every day but had little or no time to visit. He and his men were out early every morning clearing roads and bridges of land mines.

Red Cross people were surprisingly close to the front lines serving coffee and refreshments. That was a good morale booster. We stopped for coffee and doughnuts on a cold snowy day. There were three Red Cross ladies there that day. A lady about thirty years old seemed to be the leader, and the other two were in their early twenties. One was a blonde, the other a brunette. Word came to us later that the brunette lady had gotten a dishonorable discharge. She was working on the side. Before she left, she said she had enough money to buy a big ranch in Texas.

Walter and I were on a run one cold night past midnight. We had messages for an aid station near the front. We found a bird colonel doctor with a leaf colonel nurse playing cards in a tent with a bright light burning. Any kind of light is a no-no near the front. There was a bottle of scotch on the table. I gave them the mail and asked if there was any mail to go back. The bird colonel said no, but then he wanted to see my dog tags. This was not a normal thing to ask for at that time. I had never had to show my I.D. But I went to my pocket for them. Well, they started on me because they were not hanging on my neck like a good soldier. I had coveralls over my other pants and was going to my inside pocket. The colonel asked if I was drunk. I saw their bottle more than half gone, and I said I had had a sip or two. It seems he and the lady colonel had hit the scotch a little too heavily.

He called the guard and told me I would be taken to the guardhouse. As he talked, I brought my Tommy gun that was slung on my shoulder to both hands in front of me. I told him I had two more stops to make before daylight.

He said, "No, you are going nowhere."

I asked, "Do you have any mail going to Corps? Or if you want to give them a message, write it out and I will deliver it there before daylight."

The lady with him said, "Colonel,

you'd better think about this." He looked at her, then told me to go.

I walked backward to my Jeep, and we drove off. Those two were stupid. Not only were they drinking pretty heavily, but they had a bright light mighty close to the front lines. Walter and I always had a few sips along on trips; then we'd hit it a little harder after the last stop. As I look back on this situation, I have flashbacks to the orders from General Gerow: "Don't stop for anything but a freight train, destroy your Jeep and mail, and do not be captured." Gerow never said a word about stopping for someone who seemed to be showing his rank to impress a lady. He'd have to kill me if that's the way he wanted it. I would answer to God and our General.

As I look back to the early days of the Battle of the Bulge, everyone had moved back northwest from Eupen about fifty miles. Some of us didn't move from the compound where we were. We were surrounded by hills. The front lines were on these hills. Enemy units seemed to be camped in the nearby forest and filtered through under cover of night laying mines and doing more damage where they could.

One time in the first couple of weeks of the battle, we were leaving for a message run to the front. General Eisenhower and his WAC master sergeant driver had just stopped at the gate. They didn't know the password, so the gate guard wouldn't let them in. Now think about this. There are only two men of his rank in the world. The other one was in the Pacific war zone. There were also stars on a plate on the bumper. No other man in the world looked like Eisenhower except Eisenhower. And our guard wanted a password? How gung-ho can you get? The WAC master sergeant was giving her thoughts loud and clear to the guard when General Gerow noticed the situation and came walking at a fast pace. As he came by me, he gave me a sick grin and shook his head. He took care of that situation, and we were back to normal operation. A war zone is no place for gung-ho people. They do more harm than good. I don't agree with Noah Webster on his definition of *gung-ho*. My definition is a person in the armed services who doesn't have a third of the brains he thinks he has. And all his waking hours, he is a thorn in everyone's side.

There was a group of L-5 planes from the Army Air Forces with us. They took mail from Corps back to Army. Renner was fond of flying and was learning more about flying a plane every day from those pilots. One pilot named Sabo was his friend and was teaching Renner to fly on the side.

We were all friends with the pilots. When snow came, they had a problem. One pilot took the wheels off his plane and installed a pair of skis. He took off OK, but he had not gotten back when he should have. We were all worried and were there waiting for him. He made a perfect landing just before dark. Scuttlebutt was he got tied up in a bar in Paris for some reason or another and got a late start home.

We were staying on the top floor of a hotel-type building in Eupen, Belgium, late one night. One of our men brought in an automatic pistol he had found. He was showing it as his new souvenir. As it was passed around, a man from New York took hold of it with his thumb in the trigger guard and then pointed it toward his eye asking, "Is this thing loaded?" It was, and that was his last day in the war.

Back in the old home place in Texas, everyone had rifles and shotguns and almost everyone had pistols. We learned early how to handle them, and never shot ourselves or anyone else. I think that's the way it should be.

The bad days of the war came in the worst part of winter. There was snow almost every night. Troops were on the move all the time. All roads were torn up within the first week from heavy tanks and big trucks. We drove with the windshield locked down over the hood. The temperature was below freezing all the time and down near zero most every morning. We wore wool underwear and regular army issue, and I used my trading skills to get a pair of insulated coveralls used by the armored tank men. Over that I wore a mackinaw. Then there was the knit cap and helmet. The wool socks from Eleanor Roosevelt kept my feet warm. I noticed when I drove close behind a tank, the heat from its motor came out just above our Jeeps hood, and we could get warmed up.

Troops were on the move at all hours, day and night. New men came in tarp-covered trucks. These trucks had hooks on bottom of the bed to tie the tarp down with. Those hooks were just shoulder-high to me when I met the truck while I was driving a Jeep. To stay out of ditches, oncoming traffic was very close. I felt tugs at my shoulder many times as those hooks caught my mackinaw. The shoulder of it showed the wear and tear of close oncoming traffic.

The weather seemed to be the worst

around Christmastime. A large warehouse building was set up as a hospital. There were hundreds of our men in there with frozen body parts. That was not a pretty sight.

A battle to take a town comes to mind as a good example of 1st Army tactics. As I was told after the battle, the town had been shelled by artillery and bombed by the Army Air Forces to be softened up for the infantry to go in. A division of 5th Corps Infantry started in and found more resistance than expected and was pulled back out of danger. More shells and bombs were called for. The infantry tried again and were called back a second time. The stronghold was hit again with shells and bombs. After this, the 49th combat engineers went in and took the town. After they had everything pretty well under control, my friend Sergeant Tubb, Private Wilson, and another man were walking in a street. Wilson was between the other two and saw a German come up from behind a hedge with a burp gun. He swung around and shot his M1 from the hip and hit the German just above the eyes in his forehead. This saved the lives of two good friends of mine and a buddy of theirs.

I had two accidents with my Jeep in the Battle of the Bulge. One was during the first snowstorm. We were out early with five or six inches of snow on the roads. This was new to me. I came up behind a truck too fast and hit the brakes, and we were sliding under the truck bed. The wire cutter caught on the bed of the truck, and that saved us from more damage. Our mechanics had no trouble repairing our wire cutter. And they told me to reduce the tires' air pressure to fifteen or twenty pounds for better traction. As I drove off, the head mechanic told me the best way to make it on snow was to drive slower.

My other accident was also in the snow. Walter and I were on a message run through a pine forest when a German V2 rocket, or a buzz bomb, came over. One of our fighter planes caught up with it as we watched and put a wing under the buzz bomb wing and flipped it over. That messed up the mercury pilot, and the buzz bomb was on the way down. It seemed to be curving, heading to crash where we were headed. I hit the brakes too hard. Our Jeep went sideways into the ditch, turned over on its side, and kept on sliding. It went through the ditch and further on twenty or thirty yards. I was with the Jeep, but Walter was nowhere around. I kept calling out for him, but he was nowhere in sight. Then I saw him come crawling out of a snow bank. He was

OK. The buzz bomb hit and blew up maybe a half mile away. We pulled the Jeep back on its wheels, loaded the gear back in, and drove back to camp. There was no damage to the Jeep.

December has the shortest days of the year. Freezing rain and snow almost every night made driving difficult, and most of our driving was at night. Frozen roads were quickly ruined with our heavy tanks and trucks. Our army made hospitals wherever they could build tents or set up in empty buildings. Our frontline units were shifting around and being beefed up with replacements during nighttime. At times, night traffic was like downtown Dallas. Weaving in and out of traffic was normal. With priority mail, we had little time to waste. All windshields were latched over the hood. Rain and snow with cold nights and

Army traffic ruined most roads. If we were the first on the roads, night or day, there were a few "do not do" rules to go by. Good advice was: "don't drive normally."

Visiting and talking with my hometown friend Thomas Tubb taught me what to look for. He and his men were out clearing mines every day. Turn in the bar ditch not using the normal exit or drive through a barbed wire fence. Avoid culverts and bridges. Pick a path not traveled or drive across a creek if necessary.

We never knew when the Battle of the Bulge was over. It seemed to spill over into going across Germany. There could have been some politics mixed in after we reached Paris. For some reason or other, we made a fast trip northeast to Belgium. After that, everything seemed to settle down. I guessed, though, that the generals were thinking and planning for the next campaign.

As the Battle of the Bulge began to ease a little, a feeling of confidence began to build among us. Some of us began to be in Germany, mixing with the people. Most of them seemed to want to help us. Better morale comes with good news.

Waddill (standing on right) with men in his platoon

Ten: Meeting the Enemy

Our first camp in Germany was in a small village between Monschau and Ahrweiler. It is important to mention how and where we camped along the way from the beach to the end of the war. When in France, we camped out in pup tents, except in Paris, where we were in an old vacant warehouse.

From the beach to Paris, we met more resistance. The Germans were well trained and had good artillery and air strikes. We advanced more slowly and were dug in below pup tents if we were not serving forward units. After Paris, we moved faster meeting less air and artillery resistance. When in Belgium, we were billeted in vacant barns and warehouses if there were any available. The code truck was in the same compound through our early time there and through the Battle of the Bulge. They all had gas or kerosene heating. There were times when pup tents were better.

In Germany, we were in whatever was vacant at the time. The code truck had the extended tent out the back entrance any time, be it day or night. This was the best time to relax and maybe get a little sleep. First in the Czech Republic we were in office buildings and hotels. Very soon after the war we were in an old army camp which seemed to have been saved especially for us.

Word came down that there would be a fifty-dollar fine for anyone fraternizing with the Germans. A venereal disease would be absolute proof. The scuttlebutt was our Provost Marshal paid the first fine.

In Germany, we began to see more and more Gestapo-type people burning at the stake. Some were still burning. Others had the post and wood all ready for a czar they were holding. Most of our troops took the main roads across Germany. Troops were moving faster than before.

We messengers were on main highways and county roads crossing to other main roads, servicing all units. On these roads, we saw more of the home folks. Country folks seemed happy to be free from their previous German rule. I believe the regular home folks were glad to see our troops coming. Hitler had confiscated everything they had that would help run his armies. He had taken all horses and mules, and if the German farmers had tractors, they had no gas to run them. It seemed that they were glad to start new all over again.

On New Year's Day 1945, we were in a medical building east of Monschau. In the last hour of daylight, three German fighter planes came in low, strafing and bombing. Our Army Air Forces kept their front fifteen to twenty miles ahead of our ground forces. Our vehicles were parked out in plain sight. That was stupid of us, but there was no other place to park. We had maybe six inches of snow on the ground. Our fighter planes were not far behind and came on quickly. The fighters and our antiaircraft guns brought the German fighters down in a short time. One tried to crash into the building we were in but came up short and crashed a hundred yards out. We lost a good man, an antiaircraft gunner, in that raid. At the wreckage of the plane, I found a German wallet with a map and a hundred-mark note inside. I kept those things to show my grandkids.

We were in the medical building a few weeks. One day, I got choked up. A doctor checked me over and told me I had a touch of the flu or a bad cold. He wrote something on a pad and gave it to me. Then he asked me, “When did you have tuberculosis?”

I told him, “It was in the seventh grade, and I missed most of the year and had to take it over again.

He said, “You shouldn’t be here. I’m sending you home. You will be on the white boat in a week or two."

I told him, "No, I am not leaving until this war is over."

He shook his head as if to say, "Well, that is your choice."

I started back down the hall. He called, "Hey, Tex! They say you are a drinking man."

I told him, "Yeah, I do now and then."

He walked toward me and asked if maybe I had a bottle stashed away.

"Yeah," I told him, "Two bottles."

He told me to tear up that paper he had given me.

We were at my bunk. The doctor told me to get one bottle, sit on my bunk, and drink all I could as quickly as I could.

When I could hold no more, he said, "Get in bed and cover up with all the blankets you have. You will be OK in the morning. Give me the other bottle because I am not feeling well at all."

I did as he ordered and was OK and in my Jeep on a message run by 5:00 am the next day. Those Army doctors have more common sense than others. I knew this doctor had had dealings with TB sometime earlier. He was the only doctor who ever asked about my health problems. My problem was in the top area of my left lung. That part of my chest lost a year's growth. If you look closely, you can see it.

Our troops were nearing the Rhine River. Ahrweiler was on the river and was known for great wine. Walter and I were in the area on a mail run. After our last stop, we visited a winery. In the basement were six or eight large wooden barrels about eight feet in diameter. They were lined up on a long concrete shelf about three feet high. Each had a one-inch valve at the bottom. All valves were fully open, and wine was flowing to the floor. A staff sergeant was knee deep in wine at the barrel next to the wall, filling a mess cup. He was a little more than drunk.

We left and met another of our men a few blocks from there and told him, "Don't drink wine from that place. There is a sergeant wading in it."

He told us he would take care of that situation.

Walter and I found another wine store and then were on our way back to camp. I had never drunk wine before, and we both went a little overboard. I think I used the wrong words there. We went a *whole lot* overboard.

While waiting for our engineering

forces to build a bridge to cross the Rhine River, the rear had troops caught up with us and the code truck, and we were one unit again. Back at camp after a message trip to the front, we were told the mess hall was across the street and we might still be able to get something to eat. Most of our cooks were Italian, so we had spaghetti and meatballs. Walter had his mess gear. I had forgotten mine. The cook told me I did not have time to run and get it, so I put spaghetti in one pocket and meatballs in the other. When you are full of wine, most anything works.

Back with the platoon, we were all having a great time. Walter was eating from his mess gear, and I was eating out of my pockets. Our gung-ho corporal kept making remarks about my table manners. He was across the room, twenty or thirty feet away.

I picked up my mess kit and yelled, "Corporal, you gung-ho son of a bitch, you like mess kits so well, here is one!" And I threw it at him.

He dodged, but it hit him in the back of the head. My mess kit had a dent in the bottom near the handle for the remaining days of the war. All of our men were on my side and were getting a big kick out of it. They were all laughing. I went to bed shortly after that. Our gung-ho corporal came and got me up in about three hours, and put me on crap details until the bridge was finished and I moved out with Captain Bert and the forward troops again. That was my first, and last, wine deal.

Our engineers were building a pontoon bridge over the Rhine River that was said to be flowing about 15 knots. Small-arms fire was coming from the other side. Our forces were shelling and bombing the other side constantly. Our men did a good job planning and building that bridge. They had chosen a spot just downstream from a curve in the river. With that plan, they could anchor each pontoon to the shore upstream with cables. A few weeks later, we crossed that bridge. Building this bridge would not have been an easy chore in peacetime. Our men did it in combat conditions, and we owe them for the job they did.

Before we crossed the river, we were on a trip to the Ruhr pocket, several miles north of our normal line toward Berlin. Near our destination, we came to a very large field full of German prisoners. It looked like standing room only, and trucks were inside with water and rations. Scuttlebutt was that eighty thousand prisoners were taken in those battles. History now shows over two hundred thousand prisoners were taken in that area.

There was a staff sergeant at the main gate with a German officer who had just been unloaded from a truck. They seemed to be arguing. The sergeant had a rifle in his hands and gave an upper cut to the German's chin. He went down and did not get up. The handle of the sergeant's gun was broken off. One of our men dragged the German officer over by the fence, and there he lay. I would not question our sergeant for his action. With that many German prisoners in a bunch, we could not lose control. There were only a few of our guards along a normal cattle barbed wire fence. We asked directions to the office, delivered their messages, got mail, and were back in our camp before dark.

About this time in the war, our pace seemed to go faster toward Berlin. There was serious fighting among die-hard German troops. These truly hardcore German troops kept on fighting after the war in the Black Forest area, but it seemed there were a great number of the German soldiers who were ready to call it quits and go home.

We seemed to be doing more day driving. The map showed the plan of attack from Paris to Berlin in almost a straight line.

We drove through Aachen, Germany, a town of maybe five thousand that had been hit by the Army Air Forces. The whole town was leveled; not a building was standing. It must have been a hiding place for ammo or something, or our Army Air Forces would not have wiped it out.

We were near the front lines in the hill country with winding roads. Three of our P38s were in formation above. The outside one peeled off. We knew the pilot thought we were Germans in a stolen Jeep so he was coming for us. We were on a straight paved road, and we were going at a good speed. Both Walter and I knew what to do when planes were in formation and one peeled off from the other. Walter watched the plane, and I held our speed constant.

When the plane was near lining up on us, Walter said, “It’s coming at us.”

A few seconds later, I pulled the emergency brake and bailed out to the ditches. Walter did the same to the ditch on the right. The bullets from the plane went just over the Jeep on the road. When the pilot saw us shake our fists at him, he knew we weren’t Germans and didn’t come back. The secret to this situation was to speed up and then hold constant speed, then stop suddenly. The bullets would go over us and hit where we should have been. That may not be the Army way, but it worked for us. We had been strafed by both German and our own fighter planes before. Germans had only one pass; then they had to go.

During this time, one particular event in this time stands out in my mind even today, almost seventy years later. It was one of many times that I believe God sent angels to get us through safely. Walter Knight and I returned from our normal message run joining our own troops in a new bivouac area. We were in a forest near the front lines.

Stapleton came and handed me an envelope for a unit that was dug in on the front line. He said, "Tex, this is for you. It must be delivered before 11:00 pm tonight."

He gave us a hand-drawn map, an

aerial photo with roads marked that we must take to keep us out of trouble. He told us to "take the marked roads and no others." Stapleton knew we had maps that were up to date, so it was strange to get this hand-drawn map. The marked route would take us back a few miles, then north a mile or two, before going back west to our destination. On our up-to-date map, there were other roads that were shorter, but we were in a period of advancement so we were not sure where the enemy lines were.

One quick look told us that our message was to be delivered only a few miles less than an hour's drive off Hitler's new four-lane highway. I looked at Walter, and he grinned, seeing where we were headed. He said, "Let's go." We drove toward the marked route, but we turned left back toward Hitler's highway, and you know the rest of the story.

A dirt road took us over to the highway. We turned left on that nice super four-lane highway and were on our way. In about half a mile, we came upon some of our infantry. They were off on one side, sitting in the bar ditch having a chow break. They waved for us to stop. We shook our heads and kept going.

An officer in a Jeep up ahead got out and walked in front to try to stop us. I slowed down. He started to say something, and I told him we couldn't stop because we were messengers and had to go on ahead. The colonel waved both hands to go on then, shaking his head like he thought we were stupid.

We drove on a mile or two, and a dozen or more local men and women came running out from a pine tree thicket, motioning us to go back. We did not realize they were Germans living in the area who were warning us that German troops were ahead.

A couple miles further, as we topped a hill, we saw a German vehicle parked crossways in the median. There were soldiers in it. This thing looked like a command car with wheels in front and tank tracks in the rear. Walter and I looked at each other.

I said, "If we were going to get it, we would have already had it."

Walter nodded, and I drove on slowly. I will never forget what we came upon. Three German officers were in the back, sitting erect. The driver and another soldier were seated in the front. There was no top on the vehicle, and the windshield was down. The soldiers had rifles across their laps. The officers in the back wore side arms. They all seemed to be dead. I saw heat from their radiator. We stopped in front of them. I told Walter our dang infantry had probably propped them up to scare us, and we drove off.

A few miles up the road, as it curved slightly to the right, a field was on our left. The troops we were looking for should have been in the bushes across the field. We drove through the fence and headed across the field toward the bushes. A three-wire fence will break if you keep driving. We were about fifty yards from the thicket, and several of our troops came at us with guns, challenging us to halt. We halted. They were all talking at the same time, asking the password, and some were just yelling.

Just then, we heard a loud voice from the bushes saying, "Hell, that's Tex. Let him through."

They cut the fence. We drove in safe and sound before dark.

I was chewed out by all the officers there for taking a shortcut through the lines. That was nothing new; I was always being chewed out about something. All this was because of another impulse I had for a shortcut. Our unit caught up with us about noon the next day. Sergeant Stapleton wondered if we had any trouble finding this place. We told him we took a shortcut or two but had no problems.

As the years have gone by, I have seen the picture of those Germans in their vehicle over and over in my mind. There was no blood, and there were no bullet holes in the vehicle. Their uniforms were perfect. Their caps, helmets, and everything else was in place. Their heads were held erect like normal, but their eyes were closed. Did God want to keep both them and us safe? Did He make them appear to be dead? We do not know.

I will always believe the message was important and needed to be delivered "now!" Captain Bert and all of the others knew we would take the short-cut and get through. Sergeant Stapleton's tone told me that when he told me the message was for me.

Our guardian angels took us through. We were driving into that unit before dark. We knew none at that camp and a new unit joined us there. This brings up another question: Where did that voice saying, "That is Tex! Let him through" come from? I think Billy Graham once said that there were more angels fighting WWII than there were troops. I believe he was right.

One night, we were camped out in our pup tents for the night about an hour before sundown. Captain Bert came and put his gear in my Jeep and told me to get everything. We would not be coming back. I never unloaded because we very seldom went back to an old camp.

We took off toward the northeast. The roads were crowded with big trucks and heavy equipment in a convoy. The captain had arranged for a motorcycle escort through the traffic. This escort was the captain of our MP unit, and he took us through — around trucks and through ditches, with dust everywhere. We learned that a Jeep could go any place a Harley could go.

Before long, our escort was gone, and we drove on for at least two hours after dark. Then we left the main road onto a farm road and came to a farmhouse. Our battalion commander was there alone. I believe his name was Jones, though I may be wrong. He was a bird colonel. He had a Morse code system set up in the front room. He had the house set up in a blackout condition. We unloaded all of Captain Bert's stuff. I almost had all of my things in. The colonel asked me about the saddlebags, so I brought them in next. One bag held grenades. He took the other, reached in, and pulled out a bottle of moonshine. Captain Bert wondered how he knew the booze was in that bag. I told the captain that any old cavalry bird colonel knows which saddlebag the booze is in.

Captain Bert said, "Tex, don't call him a bird colonel."

The colonel told the captain, "If there is booze involved, just call me anything."

I took the rotor cap out and brought in rations. We were set up for the night. They were on the dot-dash thing and the moonshine all night. I helped them with the rations and shine for an hour or two before I bunked out for the night. As I look back now, I wonder. Were they dot-and-dashing in Navajo with our men in the Secret Service who might have been somewhere behind the front line? Our unit came and joined us about noon the next day.

Eleven: It's What the Enemy Thinks You Can Do

As we went through Germany, we drove through two places I remember. One was a town built especially to breed and raise a super race. There were apartments for specially chosen super ladies, and there were special motels for the chosen super studs. I must say the ladies did look super. We did not see the super studs.

In another town, there was a large

building that had shower stalls hooked up with gas and no water. It was not Buchenwald. It was in a small town. Andy and I stopped and went through it. We saw the shower stalls. There was an open ditch nearby with old, dried human bones and some human bodies just recently put there. We both felt there were more small towns like this for the same purpose.

On the way back to the main road through town, we turned and drove through the alley. Up in a second-story window, we saw an older woman and her daughter holding a baby. They called for us to stop. We could not speak their language, but they seemed to want us to drive around front and come up to them for dinner. We were right. They were cooking. We brought a bottle of cognac, set it on the table, and then were seated around the table. They had shot glasses, and we all got better acquainted while the food was cooking. The baby was sitting on the table and got more attention than anyone. The older lady filled the shot glasses. As I reached for one, the little baby girl caught my arm, and I saw she had her eyes on the shot glass. I looked at her mother and she was smiling, so I gave the baby a sip of cognac. She wanted another and crawled over near it and just sat there.

They were cooking regular German food, boiling some kind of meat with all kinds of vegetables in one pot on the stove. There was also coffee. As we reached for a shot of cognac for the coffee, the baby grabbed our arm for another sip. You can guess we all had a good visit. Andy seemed to really enjoy that family-type life, and I will never forget that visit. It was more like visiting with a neighbor back home. Then shortly, we were back in the war, reporting back to our camp.

One Sunday, we were on the road early. We left our last stop just past midday, driving in pretty country by a creek, and Walter remarked it would be nice to have a country Sunday dinner instead of rations. We had just passed a farm road that crossed the creek and went up to a house. We saw an older couple sitting in a porch swing. I turned around and drove to the house. The couple in the swing on the porch looked uneasy. They spoke no English, and we spoke no German. So to ease the tension, I took my gun and saddlebags and laid them on their porch, then took a can of gas and set it by their car. They began to smile. Walter took spirits from the Jeep, and we were welcome. When I mentioned Texas and names of German families from back home, they got excited. They took us in the kitchen and started cooking and showing us pictures of their two sons in the service. They told us not to shoot their boys. You can guess the rest. We all had a wonderful time and had found new friends. As we drove away, the couple were standing on the front porch waving to us like, "Y'all come back sometime."

We came to a town just at sundown. All the natives were gone. We went into a house with food cooking on the stove. We had a good dinner. Someone found champagne in the cellar, and we had a champagne party that night. We took three cases with us as we broke camp before daylight. As we drove, we came upon a convoy of new replacements going to the front. One of the men in the last truck saw the champagne and wanted some. Walter got out on our hood and held on to the wire cutter, and we passed bottles to him to hand on to the men in the truck as we drove. Every man in the truck got a bottle. We drove on around the convoy and never knew what outfit those men were going to. When they reached their new unit, I bet their sergeant was proud of his new replacements.

The war was changing. Most of the enemy seemed to believe the war was near the end. It seemed we were going through more territory a lot faster than before.

Once we were in a German's house for the night. People seemed to know we were coming and would walk out and hide someplace and leave their houses open for us. One of our men found a wall safe which he couldn't open it. The group stood back and shot it with armor piercing bullets until it came open. They found a collection of old coins. One of them dated back to the 1500s. It was not round and was about the size of a silver dollar. It had eight or ten sides and was in good condition. I never noticed any of the others. There was a shoebox more than half full of coins. I didn't know the man who kept them. There was no man of rank among us that night. To me, those men were just plain stealing.

Walter and I stopped at a match factory to just look at the place. No one was there. There was a yard full of match stems on the ground. A bobtail truck with cattle sideboards loaded with guns of all kinds drove up and stopped. The driver got out. He was German but could speak English. As we looked at the guns, he told us to take anything we wanted. A truckload of guns Hitler had taken from the people and take anything we wanted? What a deal. I noticed a big game over-and-under shotgun rifle. It was covered with silver plates of birds on one side and big game on the other. I wrapped it in a shelter half tent, and it lay perfectly along the left side of the driver's seat in my Jeep. I ended up trading that gun to a Russian soldier for a bottle of vodka in our end of war celebration in Plzeň, Czechoslovakia. Man, did I take him in that trade?

Sergeant Hertz was our code man, and he was the best. He was a German of Jewish descent. His father had been a university professor and had sent Hertz and his mother to New York several years earlier. His father was gassed by Hitler.

Early one morning, Hertz came with mail and told me he would be going on that trip. He gave me directions as I drove. I had no clue where we would end up, but I knew we were near the front lines. We came up to a bridge across a small creek. It was cement, and the road was blacktop. A gravel road off to the right was a bypass to a wooden bridge crossing down below. This was just before sunup. I thought: *We may be the first to cross the bridge this morning*. I remembered the training films back at Camp Crowder basic training and took the warning. I backed up about a hundred yards and drove off into the ditch near the fence. With front wheel drive, I forded the creek and got back on the highway a half-mile past the creek. Sergeant Hertz told me I was crazy; we could have taken the gravel road across the wooden bridge.

We drove into the town Hertz said was Naumburg, where our troops were going house to house. The sergeant directed me to a residential area. We stopped in front of a house in the block adjoining a university campus. He said that was his father's house where he was born. We saw a lady with two boys at the end of the block at the campus. She was watching our troops go building to building across campus. She came walking toward us with a kid on each side. They were maybe three or four years old and were wearing German air-force-type clothes. As she came by, she saw the sergeant and quickly turned, took a step toward us, and stood looking down at him sitting in the Jeep. I will never forget the look in her eyes. It did not seem to be hate; it was more like fire. She did not take her eyes off him for a very long moment. She never spoke a word, nor did the sergeant. Then she turned abruptly and walked her kids into the house next door. Sergeant

Hertz just sat there, looking straight ahead for a short time. Then he motioned me to drive on. When we stopped at the corner, he told me that had been his childhood sweetheart. He never mentioned her again. Sergeant Hertz had been born there and probably had many friends in that area.

We delivered our mail and were on the road back. We noticed my hometown friend Sergeant Tubb with his engineers at the creek bridge. He told us his men had cleared the bridge of mines, and it was now OK to drive over. As we drove over, we saw that a big army truck had taken the gravel road to the right and had run over a land mine near the edge of the blacktop. The left front wheel of the truck was blown off.

Sergeant Hertz looked at me and said, "This is why we ford creeks." He learned really quickly.

We knew the war was almost over. Our whole world seemed to be more at ease. We no longer felt the pressure of being in a war. We had turned south off our straight shot toward Berlin a few days earlier.

Our first sergeant Mac came up with us to stay a day or two. Someone had brought a German motorcycle into camp. He got on it and took off down a gravel road. When he rounded a curve, he met a squad of German soldiers. He had no gun. Both Sergeant Mac and the Germans were more or less in shock. The sergeant stopped, got off the motorcycle, and yelled at them to come to attention. They did. He then yelled at them to drop their guns, and they did. Then he commanded them to march in front of him as he came into camp on their motorcycle. No one knew what to do with his prisoners, so we all sat down together and had C-rations.

I was driving Lieutenant Wilson back to his quarters, and he made a remark that I should have taken that opportunity to be an officer. It would have been easier than driving a Jeep. I thought he had been drinking. I did not know anything about the opportunity he mentioned. But I had a flashback to the West Point officer, and that was probably what he was speaking of. I didn't want it when I became a private first class. All I wanted was to get the war over and go back home.

We were in a town for a few days; I guess the brass was figuring out what to do next. With nothing much to do, we were driving around the town, just looking. We found a dirt racetrack that was a half or three-quarters around and had slightly elevated corners. In a short time, there were about six of us going around and around, just test-driving. Shortly after that, we had gas and oilcans along the front side for pit stops. Our Jeeps were all lined up, ready to go. We started slow and then began to race. We made several laps of good racing, bumping one, then another now and then. I don't know who was in the lead.

At the finish line was Sergeant Stapleton standing in his weapons carrier. We stopped, and when the dust cleared, our sergeant was cussing and chewing us out for running our Jeeps like that. As he cooled off a little, he told us we didn't have any business being on a racetrack and that he could outrun any of us in his weapons carrier.

We were all quiet for a short minute, and I heard someone say, "You can't outrun a turtle with your truck."

One thing led to another, and we were all on the track running at full speed. Dust was a half-mile high.

After a few laps, there was a command car parked at the finish line, and Captain David, our company commander, was standing in front of it. We all knew the race was over and stopped. We were all lined up with our sergeant near the front. The captain just stood there and never said a word, but he looked at us for what seemed like forever. Then he got in his car and drove quietly away. He did not say a word, and I believe that was the best chewing out on record. We gathered all of our equipment and went back to camp. I still believe I won.

A few days later, we camped in a small town. A train was steamed up and ready to roll near the railroad station. One of our cooks had worked for a railroad. He put the train in reverse and went backwards out of sight. In a half hour or so, here he came back with a trainload of German prisoners. If he could do that, it seemed to me it was time to stop the war and we should all go home.

Scuttlebutt was that Hitler had shot himself and his woman had taken the pill. We thought this had taken place at his underground hiding place in the mountains.

We were moved into Plzeň, Czechoslovakia, on May 5, 1945. Renner and I went out of town to the airport. Renner had learned to fly. The German Stork was the same as our Cub airplane. Before I knew what was going on, he had that Stork in the air. I saw our troops just coming in. I drove around telling them, "Don't shoot! That is one of our stupid men up in that airplane!"

The natives were decked out in loud,

flowery parade-type clothing. The parade celebrating the end of the war started later that day. Andy and I joined in behind them. That didn't last long. The people pulled us out for drinks along the sidewalk. This went on all day and most of the night, well after the parade ended.

The next morning, Andy and I found ourselves in my Jeep down a bomb crater. The sun was shining and the birds were singing. Back at our camp, we found everyone else had the same hangover. I had traded my African hunting rifle to a Russian for a quart of vodka and had most of it left. That was good. It is better to have some left for morning recuperation.

This was the sixth of May. We turned all our guns and grenades back to supply. They moved us into a city hall-type building, which had restrooms with showers.

The cooks were set up close by. This was a day of rest and was the first day our company had all been together since England. Mostly we were all trying to get mail off to folks back home saying that we were OK.

I had driven my Jeep just over 29,000 miles. We had been in combat 336 days. The road from the beach to Plzeň, Czechoslovakia, through France and Belgium was about 1,300 miles.

As I look back at the war across Germany, we seemed to be going at a faster pace than before. We reached the largest town in eastern Czechoslovakia a few hours before the Russian troops got there. The Russian lines were just outside of town. U.S. troops had a corner of the Czech Republic. This may have given the Czechs a better chance of freedom than they might have had with Russia.

The German country people we had contact with seemed to be glad to see us coming. There were times as we entered towns that families had walked out and left food cooking on their stove. That seemed to be a welcome sign. The food was good. Normally we would bunk on the floor and leave early the next morning.

I remember driving by a farm and seeing an orchard with ripe peaches or some other fruit. We stopped and were at a tree looking for ripe fruit, so we didn't see the farmer and his wife and kids coming out. As we did, we started walking back to our Jeep with no peaches or anything. The old farmer stopped us and jabbered on in German while his wife and kids filled two buckets of their fruit and put them in our Jeep. We had found new friends among the enemy, and they seemed to be glad the war was winding down.

The German army was on the run. They were like us. They just wanted to get the war over with and go home. Although there was resistance, most of the die-hard German soldiers were headed for cover in the Black Forest. Months after VE Day, we were kept in Czech and tent cities in France. Scuttlebutt was that union workers in America were on strike and would not unload boats leaving or coming in. The war was over, but we were cooling our heels because of a labor union back home.

The war was over for us in Europe. We turned our guns in. The .30-caliber machine gun was like new. We never loaded it. I never even attended .30-caliber loading school. Along with it came three or four boxes of bullets that we also returned. They gave us six hand grenades; we returned five. (Remember, Frankie threw one to see what it would do.) And we returned the two incendiary grenades. We never needed to destroy the mail or Jeep. And the Tommy gun with ammo was also returned. We used it a few times to shoot at German planes as they were strafing us, but we missed. We had been glad to have those guns because they made us look mean, and that was good. So in a war it is not what we do; it is what the enemy thinks we can do that counts.

Twelve: Sometimes It Gets Worse Before It Gets Better

Early on the morning of May 7th Sergeant, Stapleton came in with Sergeant Hertz. I knew something was coming down.

Stapleton said, "Tex, I have orders, and you are the one to go."

The orders were from Captain Bert and the message was from General Eisenhower to the Czech government and Russian Generals who were all in Prague.

He told me Sergeant Sweeney had my guns and grenades ready and was mounting my 30-caliber. We were warned there could be troops that have not got the word that the war was over. Three others were going. Sergeant Hertz could speak German, one private could speak Czech, and another private could speak Russian. I had trouble with English, but I could get by.

We found the Russian lines about a mile northeast of Plzen. The guards let us through. We were on gravel roads and had driven about thirty miles in a slow drizzle of rain when we met a Russian military car. Marshal Tito was in the rear seat of that car, and he wanted to know where we were going and why. Sergeant Hertz told him we were on a mission for Eisenhower to Prague. Then he wanted to know if Eisenhower was in Plzen. We didn't know. They drove off a few yards then back to us. Marshal Tito told us to be sure to get a return message from the Russians to Eisenhower or we would never get back through the Russian lines.

Waddill (left) with Sgt. Hertz (2nd to left) & his two men

5th Corps Headquarters moving into Plzen as the war ended in May 1945.

About ten miles further we rounded a curve and met at least three platoons of German soldiers. They must have seen us coming.

They were lined across the road, the front row kneeling, and they all had their guns on us, point blank. An officer came and stood to my left and facing us. In broken English, he said they had word that the war may be over.

Sergeant Hertz in German told him that is true; the war is over. We heard a murmur among the soldiers and saw them began relaxing with their guns. The officer said, “Well then, you are not our prisoners; we are your prisoners. What would you have us do?”

Sergeant Hertz told them, “Stack your guns and go home.”

We heard a lot of yelling with joy as they stacked their guns, and we drove on.

At the headquarters in Prague, there were Czech men dressed in suits and Russian generals all in the room. The

Russians seem to have the upper hand because they took the messages and seemed to disregard them. We asked for a reply to Eisenhower. They said there would not be one and for us to leave. Then Sergeant Hertz told them that Marshal Tito told us to be sure to get a return message from them to Eisenhower.

They talked among themselves and then seemed to get in a better humor. One of the Russian generals wrote something on paper, put it in an envelope marked for Eisenhower and gave it to Sergeant Hertz. One of them asked if we want to go sight-seeing in the old historical town.

Hertz nodded okay.

They sent the chief of police as a guide. Among other things we saw the old Kings Church that is over a thousand years old. You wouldn't believe the worn trails in the stone floors or worn handholds on backs of hard wood pews. These worn seats were evidence of hundreds of people over hundreds of years using the pew in front of them to sit down and get up again. There were tombs dated over twelve hundred years ago in a cellar below.

That church is what I remember most. Now as I remember that old church, I see a dark stone church building with vines growing to the roof. There was a sun dial on a stool about 10 yards from the front door in the yard. To me, that church had to be some kind of link between early men of God like Abraham and Moses and us back-sliding Methodists who carried moonshine in their saddlebags. As we drove around, we saw a large number of American prisoners that had just been released. We took the guide back to their headquarters.

As we were leaving, we saw an American soldier on the sidewalk near what seemed be the town square. We stopped. He came over and said he was from Ohio. We told him he could go back with us; otherwise he may not get through the Russian lines.

He said, “Man, we are American. We will get home okay, and besides that, they are having a big ball for us tonight. We will be in all the bars celebrating.”

As we left town, we saw hundreds of German and a few more of our men who just seemed to be wandering around. Without the return message written by the Russians, their guards would not have let us back through their lines to rejoin our own troops.

Our guns were again returned back to supply. As we told our stories about that trip, they all wanted to go see Prague. We told them they could get through the lines okay, but they could not get back. Scuttlebutt was that a few men went the next day and were never seen again.

The next day was the 8th of May. The generals all met, and the war was over. Word was that some wanted to send our unit to the Pacific, but Eisenhower refused and let us go home.

Three or four days later an officer we'd never seen before came by and said, "Which one of you is Tex?"

I nodded.

He told me to get my guns from supply. Then he added that we were going to Austria for a couple of days.

I thought, *Man, the war is over. When is this going to let up?*

We drove through Munich. That town had been bombed out; our Army Air Forces and probably our artillery had leveled every building we drove by. Workers were using large shovels and trucks to clean everything up in order to start rebuilding. On further south, we came on the trail that Hannibal took with the elephants. I'd never seen any other mountains to compare with those.

We stopped at a very large lake. There was one large building like a park headquarters or restaurant. No one was there. The officer told me there were at least two divisions of die-hard German soldiers in the Black Forrest across the lake. We didn't lose much time there.

Shortly we were headed south. The road seemed to take us off the top of a hill. We casually noticed a sign saying use first gear. Very soon after that, I realized if the sign says first gear, it is time to go to first gear, not second gear. I tried second gear and knew right off that first gear or lower would have been a better choice. We reached the bottom of the hill in record time. On the way down I looked at the officer, and he was calm and collected as though this is everyday life.

We stopped in a town just seven miles north of the Brenner Pass. I never knew why the trip was made. The officer may have been working in G2 where all the secrets are kept in our part of the army.

Just east of this town was a very high cliff. They told us a golf course was on top of that cliff. A small cub-type airplane was in the air near the top. We were told the pilot was still trying to fly to the top and land near the golf course. He didn't make it that day. We were there only one day before we headed back to Czechoslovakia. On the trip back, we passed a convoy of our troops on their way north.

When we got back to camp, I returned all of the war gear back to supply for the last time. I had been through five campaigns: Normandy, Northern France, Ardennes, Rhineland, and Central Europe. That was my last wartime trip.

We moved to an army base on the north side of town. Lieutenant Engel became a Captain and our new company commander. I was proud for him; he was a good officer and friend. Burke came, and he was happier than I had ever seen him. He was joining the 49th combat engineers and was on the way to their camp in hills to the southeast several miles. There were several thousand Germans holding out in those hills. I was glad for him but couldn't figure out what he was thinking. The war was over.

Captain Engel came and gave me a

shirt with two stripes and told me I was his new corporal. I told him I didn't want to be a corporal. All I wanted to do was catch a ride back to Texas. He told me to take it and go home later. Well, I did not want the job, and I had no idea how to do it. I had not seen corporals do much of anything. I kept doing the things like every day army life. The Jeep was still mine, and we made message runs when we were called on to do so.

Everyone with eighty-five or more points was on the way home. I had eighty-four points. Points were given for time in service and medals. I was having coffee with Thomas Tubb at the Red Cross. He had eighty-four points, too. I mentioned that if I had taken that Purple Heart for those stiches, that would have given me five more points, and I would've been on the way home. He said he had used five first aid kits coming up the hill on D-Day and several more in his normal work. He had no aid station there to go to and no Purple Heart.

One morning, one of our new men and I parked in front of the Red Cross and were walking in for coffee. We met an old friend, the captain of the Military Police.

I greeted him "Hi, Captain," as he walked on toward the door.

He got me by the arm and started with all that spit and polish stuff like back at Camp Crowder. I saw he was writing something on a pad and began telling me I was out of uniform. He said that I should have been wearing my helmet liner rather than holding it under my arm.

All the time he was writing, I was telling him what I thought of a fellow like him. I thought this is the last straw; he and I had worked and drove together several times all through the war. When I paid the bird colonel the twenty-dollar fine, I asked him if this would help build their new swimming pool. He didn't smile. He just pointed toward the door. The world had changed overnight, and I suddenly didn't like this kind of army.

We had nearly all new men and were busy showing them their new duties. All men in Europe with more than eighty-five points were on stand-by to go home. We had just finished 336 days of combat on duty 24 hours a day. Add in another year in England on duty all daylight hours with a couple of weekends in a near-by town for less than a dollar a day. The majority of our troops could add two to three more years to that in England.

One Saturday afternoon, Bagwell wanted to ride out and see the country. I had a Jeep checked out, so we left for the farming area. We were out about twenty or thirty miles in farm country and were driving through a very small town. There were several people at a building like a community center. I pulled over and stopped.

A nice-looking blonde lady came over to my side and said, "The other fellow should be driving," speaking good English. She went on to say that there were more stripes on my sleeve than his. She was the only one there that could speak English, so she told us there were five or six German soldiers that had come home and were still in uniform. There was going to be a big party to celebrate in that community center. There would be food, beer, and a band for dancing. She asked us to stay for a while and join the fun.

The whole community seemed to be already there or on the way there. We took the rotor cap out of our Jeep and went inside to join the crowd. The blond was named Margaret; she was from Leipzig, Germany. Her dad ran the depot there, and she was staying with her uncle who lived up the street and farmed just out of town. Her father had moved her there to be out of the war. Everyone did a lot of talking, and when Bagwell called me "Tex," there was a lot more to talk about.

A couple of the soldiers came and asked through Margaret if we would take our Jeep and go with them to get more beer kegs from farmhouse cellars. I asked if they could drive a Jeep. They nodded, and I handed them the rotor and told them if they would go alone, they could bring more beer. Everyone thought that was nice of me to trust them with a Jeep. The party broke up after midnight. When we took Margaret home only a block away, she wanted us to come back the next afternoon. That seemed like the right thing to do.

The next afternoon we drove up to a wooded area for a picnic. We had a fire going, and we talked till midnight. Then we went home. They had a dance every Saturday night. I began to spend all of my spare time with our new friends.

Captain Engel wanted me to be the platoon sergeant. I told him no; I did not want the job. He said we would talk about it later but in the mean time I would be doing that job. One Sunday I went to the motor pool and discovered one of our trucks was gone. There was one man missing. I knew he had a sweetheart at a farm about three miles out.

I found him and the truck out in the field helping the girl's dad get his wheat crop in the barn. They told me Hitler had taken all his horses and mules. His daughter was there, and she could speak English, so she did the talking. I told our man to go on with the wheat hauling if he was not busy and to bring the truck back to the motor pool at night.

We got word that Burke, who had become a sniper, had been shot out of a tree, and now he was dead. We never knew any more than that. It was bad news and not easy to take. He and I had boarded the train together leaving Camp Crowder. When I had time and saw him in the field, I would stop and visit. He never talked much about family or where he was raised. Most of all it seemed to me he was always pushing to do something more than he was doing, but I never knew why. What more could he do than what he did? The war had been over more a month, and he was gone.

Captain Engel came by and wanted to know if I would go along with a vote to get a new sergeant. I agreed and got all the votes except one because I voted for Maynard. Being a sergeant was not a good thing for me. I had no idea how to do the job, and all I wanted was to get back to Texas.

I told the men, "If you want me to be the boss, then that is what I will be - the boss. You can all sleep in tomorrow."

We did and spent two weeks with broom handles that had a nail in one end picking up anything that was not growing. This duty was only for when we had nothing else going. That is for everyone except me. I was to be there every day. This was the first time I had news of our new First Sergeant. I didn't know he was the gung-ho corporal I had helped look for me for three weeks on the ship as we sailed to England. Sometimes things just don't work out for the better; sometimes things get worse.

Thirteen: When the War Was Finally Over

This First Sergeant, whose name I still don't remember, had me on detail to drill the company the next Saturday on the drill field. I had no idea how do that. I marched them out toward the drill field. One of my men came after me in my Jeep as I had instructed him to do and told me there was a problem at message center.

I told my new First Sergeant, "Duty

calls," and left. My new man and I went for coffee at the downtown Red Cross.

I had gone on a message run just to get out of camp and got word that the young man who had the farm girl friend had wrecked his Jeep and was in a hospital near-by. At the hospital I saw he was not hurt too bad. I knew he was out with a Jeep unauthorized, and he was in trouble. I was out legal, so I erased my Jeep number and mileage and replaced those with his. Then I gave him my trip ticket to make him legal. Back at the motor pool, I made a new trip ticket, so I was legal also. Our new gung-ho First Sergeant thought he had me dead to right this time. He was carrying a grin that would not quit until the papers all got to Captain Engel's desk.

Captain Engel told me later, "Tex, you did a good job handling that situation."

I was one up on the new First Sergeant. Again.

One morning I was in front of Captain Engel's office when he was just reporting in for work. He stopped and buttoned my coat and straightened my shirt collar.

Then he said, "You never did want to be a soldier, did you?"

I told him we did the job we came to do and now "let's all go home."

I believe Captain Engle put my name in the pot to be shipped home that day. This was a couple of months after the Generals signed a cease-fire.

Captain Engel brought in another sergeant. Helping him and several new men into the daily operation was routine for me. This kept us busy only a few hours every morning. I was spending more time with my lady friend in the farmlands several times a week. She was my same age, and I was getting real fond of her. She was about five feet, eight inches tall and was built like a brick outhouse. Her Dad had a job for me on the railroad at Leipzig Germany any time I needed work, or she would come to Texas as soon as I could get home and find a job. That was what we talked about the most. We were in the piney woods picnicking or just sitting by a campfire most of the time. Back home, my folks moved to California. I didn't care to settle any place except Texas, but I didn't want to go back to my old job near Houston. I was really happy with my girlfriend and all of our friends. I knew I wasn't going to stay in the Army. Why would anyone want the army life if there was no war? Spit polish was not my thing. It was just not right to say "sir" and salute someone who was a stranger to me.

About six months went by before word came in that we were shipping out. I had papers filled out to get out of the army and stay with a job in Germany. I went to the Colonel's office to get him to sign them. He was Colonel Bogus, a man I had known since he was a Lieutenant and had thought of him as one of the best officers in the company.

He said, "Tex, I won't sign this."

Man, I lost it and started cussing. He turned around and put his feet up on the window and waited until I finished.

When I got through, he turned back around and said, "Tex, I have read all of your mail coming and going. And you are going home. What you do after that is your business." Then he handed me papers and told me to be on the train that was leaving at about four in the morning.

I took the papers and drove out to the farmland. My lady was dressed like she was ready for a party. We visited with the family, and most of the town folk came by to wish me a good trip home. I left about 2:00 a.m. I really cared for the lady and every one in that town; they were just like home folks. Driving back to camp, I was sure I would be back soon. Things did not work out, and the trip back was not to be.

At 4:00 a.m., I was on the train in a boxcar with about forty others headed toward France. First we were in tent cities. After a few days, we were taken to an army base near the southern coast of France.

I noticed on the bulletin board a note with a message that read "*Sergeant Waddill is Sergeant of the Guard tonight.*" I reported in with the other men at the guardhouse about 6:00 p.m., just before sundown. The Officer of the Day was not there at that time,

Troops starting the journey home after the war.

and we saw no evidence of guns or ammo. Stand guard without guns or ammo? I thought not. So we began playing Hearts. I was wearing a coat with no Sergeant Stripes on the sleeves. The Officer of the Day came in and saw us playing cards and inquired if any of us had seen Sergeant Waddill.

I said, "They call me Tex. And, no, we have not seen him."

He left and came by a couple more times until around midnight and did not come by any more. The card game broke up about 4:00 a.m. I went to my bunk to take a nap before breakfast, and there was someone in my bunk.

I shook him and said, "Hey, buddy! You're in my bunk."

It was the Officer of the Day. He looked at me said, "You son of a bitch. I thought it was you all the time."

I told him that worked for me all through the war, and it seemed to come to me naturally.

He looked at his watch and said, "The cooks should be up by now. Let's have breakfast."

We had a good visit. As he left to go to his quarters, he wished me good luck on the trip home.

I was in line to board the Fayetteville Victory ship. I saw a Sergeant with a bulldog in his arms going up the steps to board the ship. The one time I had seen him before he and his dog were in a Jeep next to mine D-Day on the landing barge. I was glad the Sergeant and his dog made it through the war okay, and I wondered whether or not the dog had learned to shoot the side mount .30-caliber machine gun.

We were a group of men from all units transferred into the 78th division and were being sent home. The group with me was mostly from the 101st Airborne. Years later we noticed in the Ripley's *Believe It or Not* section of the daily news that he bailed out in combat holding his dog in his arms. It takes all kinds to fight a war; even dogs help some.

We were aboard the Fayetteville Victory ship and sailed out. The sea was calm. We passed the Rock of Gibraltar, and the sea was as smooth as silk. As we began to see nothing but water, there were about twenty men in line to get a haircut. A new friend and I joined in. We were second and third in line when we hit rough seas. A few minutes later the barber got sick. That was the end of that. This new friend and I were among very few others who were not seasick.

Visiting with him as we had coffee in the shortly vacated mess hall, he mentioned he was in a tank outfit in the war. Soon the mess hall was full of men who were not affected by rough seas, but the cooks were sick. We had to make our coffee and cook our breakfast. There were those among us who were good at cooking.

My friend talked about his family and told me he could see out of only one eye since he was very young. He was 44 years old. He had a wife and seven kids back home. He joined the army during the hard times of the drought. He had crawled out of seven tanks that were burning or knocked out and mounted another and kept going. When I learned what others had done, it makes what I did seem like a drop in a bucket compared to them.

We had rough seas only a day or two. It was reported the ship's captain turned frail and pale and disappeared toward his quarters in those rough waves. Smooth sailing brought almost every one back to the top deck. After that we had a very good trip to the shores of America.

We landed at New Port News, Virginia. Our group was among the last to unload. We were on one side of a street not in formation, but we were all lined up in step headed home. On the other side, there was a group of new men in formation. They were not in step headed toward the boat to ship out.

Near the ship dock, we were taken to a camp of army-type buildings for the night, so we could catch a train the next day for home. I knew no one there.

I told the man in the next bunk, "They call me 'Tex.'"

He said, "They call me 'Mo.'"

"Does that 'Mo' stand for Montana?" I asked.

He said he didn't know for sure.

I asked what was next on the program.

He mentioned the liquor store he had seen down the street.

I said, “Let’s go!”

The natives told us there is a club nearby. We could get food, but we had to bring our own refreshments. We did and found a table near the band. There was dancing and we could order food. Drinks were on us. There were two to three hundred people in that hall-type building.

The food was good, and the band played on. In the war, we did not drink liquor; we sipped it. Drinking the strong American liquor was a new world I was not accustomed to after the weaker homemade stuff we got used to in Europe.

Mo disappeared and never came back. I asked everyone I met if they had seen Mo. That caught on and everyone began to call out, “Has any one seen Mo?”

Later an officer stood me up on the table where he and his wife were. All was quiet at that moment, and he yelled out, "All together now… *Has anyone seen Mo?*"

Then they all said, "No!"

Not long after that, I become aggravated at everyone and went up on the stage. I shut the band down and started telling everyone over the microphone what I thought of them. My language would not be proper in our old Methodist Church back home. The military police came in every door. A group of airborne troops in my unit came and took me out the back door. In the dark, they were all around me so the military police would not see me. After that they took me to my bunk. The next day we were on the train headed for Texas. I never saw Mo again.

I got off a bus at the station in San

Antonio with army bags of clothing and a few souvenirs and a small case with personal stuff in it. A Red Cap told me he would help me with the large bag. He took them and said he would take them around the other side of the bus to load it for me. I never saw the bag or him again. I would bet he owned an army surplus store around the corner.

A Sergeant at Fort Sam Houston told us that if we wanted out of the army today we could sign up for another three years in the reserve. The other choice was to stay around and get mustered out in a few days. I signed up for three years reserve and left the army that day.

I had been through a war, hit the beach with the first wave going in with the First Infantry Division, and was the last in my outfit to turn my guns in. I had helped fight a war, but I was never a soldier and had no desire to be one.

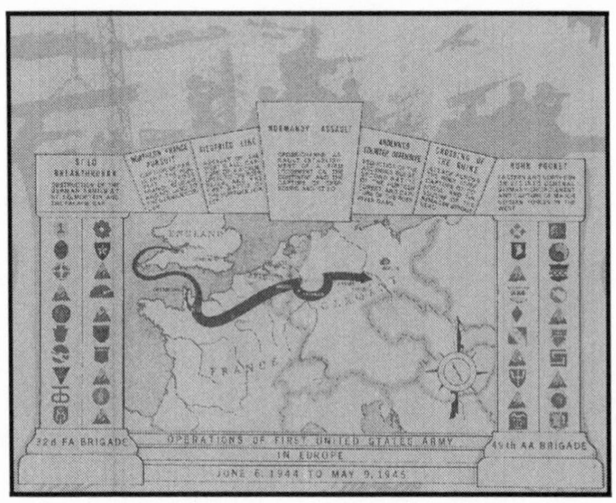

Operations of the 1st U.S. Army in Europe

Seeing old friends back where I worked before the war was good. They wanted me to go back to work and later go to a university and become a civil engineer. That didn't seem the right way to go. Seeing and visiting with old friends was good but short-lived. My folks were in California, and that is where I needed to be. In California I had a few months training as a Chevrolet mechanic; then I worked a few months. Soon after that, we all came back to Texas.

Army of the United States

HONORABLE DISCHARGE

THIS IS TO CERTIFY THAT Norris H Waddill 38 414 368 Sergeant Headquarters Company 3d Battalion 291st Infantry

ARMY OF THE UNITED STATES is hereby Honorably Discharged from the military service of the United States of America. This certificate is awarded as a testimonial of Honest and Faithful Service to this country.

Given at Separation Center Fort Sam Houston, Texas

S C Mays

Date 2 December 1945

Major Inf

Waddill Norris H. — 38 414 368 — Sgt — Inf — AUS

Headquarters Company 3d Battalion 291st Infantry — 2 Dec 45 — Separation Center Fort Sam Houston Texas

Gen Del Ireland Coryell Co., Texas — 21 Dec 22 — Ireland Texas

See 9 — Brown — Black — 6'1" — 183 — 0

X — X — X — Instrument Man Surveying 0-54.300

MILITARY HISTORY

30 Jan 43 — - - — 8 Feb 43 — Ind Sta Houston Texas

X — 1 — Brazoria Co., Texas — See 9

Messenger Dispatcher 675 — Sharpshooter Rifle 11 Mar 43

Normandy Northern France Ardennes Rhineland Central Europe GO 33 WD 45

EAME Campaign Medal with 5 Bronze Stars & Bronze Arrowhead; Good Conduct Medal; Bronze Star Medal GO 76 Hq V Corps 21 Jun 45; Victory Medal; 4 Overseas Service Bars

None

25 Feb 45 — 5 Apr 45 — 23 Apr 45 — Typhus 19Apr45 — 21 Oct 43 — NAME — 2 Nov 43

0 — 8 — 29 — 2 — 1 — 4 — Sgt — 13 Nov 45 — US — 24 Nov 45

None

Convenience of the Government (RR 1-1 Demobilization) AR 615-365 15 Dec 44

None — 8 — 4 — 0

PAY DATA

2 — 10 — 3 — 300 — 100 — none — 13.25 — $50.00 cash 233.03 check — W.A. Whittet Lt Col FD

INSURANCE NOTICE

X — X — Dec 31 — Jan 2 — 6.50 — X

Honorable discharge papers made Tex a civilian once again.

Eight million men were out looking for a work. There were no jobs left. That six-month delay caused by the union dockworkers hit us hard. One day I was helping load out lumber in a small south

Texas town doing odd jobs. I was at a streetlight waiting to cross and go for coffee. A Padre came up beside me. He wore cowboy boots, Levi Straus jeans, a Stetson hat, and a white collar.

He looked over asked me, “Well, Tex, did you ever find Mo?”

I shook my head and told him I was still looking.

Later, before I left that town I saw him in the café. He was having apple pie with a scoop of ice cream on top and a bottle of beer. I knew then the war was over and everything was getting back to normal in Texas.

I found odd jobs here and there, but never anything I was satisfied with. After about eighteen months, I finally found a job with a major oil company. When I took the physical for employment, the doctor only looked at my throat and checked my pulse. His report to the oil company was that I had TB and my kidneys were no good. I didn't get the job, and I didn't understand why. With the examination he gave me, how could that doctor make that report?

Those were my worst days. I left South Texas. I thought with my health problems I would go back home for a while. Then maybe I'd go west and get a job on a ranch and forget about a family of my own. There was a letter from my lady in Czechoslovakia. She was waiting for word to come to Texas, but I knew I couldn't go back if I had to fight medical doctors to work for a major company. I never wrote her again.

Waddill receiving the Bronze Star

During the war, I received several decorations and citations: European-African-Middle Eastern (EAME) Campaign Medal with 5 Bronze Campaign Stars & Bronze Arrowhead for D-Day, Good Conduct Medal, Bronze Star Medal, Victory Medal, General Citation, and four bars showing two years duty overseas.

But in a war, many things happen that we have no control over. I did some things I wasn't proud of, and I let some things happen that I had control of but didn't stop. These things ate deep in my soul. I talked to God many times, but that didn't help. Then one day, as I stepped up on a loading dock to get wire to load on a truck, I held my palms out and looked toward the heavens and asked God what more could I do. I felt the flutter of a white dove on each shoulder, and a chill came down through my body all the way down to bottom of my feet. At that moment, I knew the war was over for me.

I had never wanted to be a soldier. I had just wanted to serve my country and fight for what was right. I did my job, followed my impulses, and made it through World War II, shooting from the hip.

Waddill in 1948

Waddill in 2008